D1311368

The Lucent Library of Historical Eras

The 1960s
Life on the Front Lines:
The Fight for Civil Rights

Michael V. Uschan

LUCENT
BOOKS®

THOMSON

GALE

San Diego • Detroit • New York • San Francisco • Cleveland • New Haven, Conn. • Waterville, Maine • London • Munich

© 2004 by Lucent Books. Lucent Books is an imprint of The Gale Group, Inc.,
a division of Thomson Learning, Inc.

Lucent Books® and Thomson Learning™ are trademarks used herein under license.

For more information, contact
Lucent Books
27500 Drake Rd.
Farmington Hills, MI 48331-3535
Or you can visit our Internet site at http://www.gale.com

ALL RIGHTS RESERVED.
No part of this work covered by the copyright hereon may be reproduced or used in anyform or by
any means—graphic, electronic, or mechanical, including photocopying, recording, taping, Web dis-
tribution, or information storage retrieval systems—without the writtenpermission of the publisher.

LIBRARY OF CONGRESS CATALOGING-IN-PUBLICATION DATA

Uschan, Michael V., 1948–
    Life on the front lines : the fight for civil rights / by Michael V. Uschan.
      v. cm.— (Lucent library of historical eras)
Includes bibliographical references and index.
Contents: A decade of revolt against racism—Preacher power: Black ministers lead the
fight—Sit-ins: young people fight for their rights—Freedom riders: integrating interstate travel—Voter registration: the fight for the right to vote—Black power: a new militancy for blacks—White backlash: resisting the civil rights movement—Black pride: a
new mood sweeps the nation.
    ISBN 1-59018-387-8 (hardback : alk. paper)
    1. African Americans—Civil rights—History—20th century—Juvenile literature. 2. Civil
rights movements—United States—History—20th century—Juvenile literature. 3. United
States—History—1961–1969—Juvenile literature. [1. African Americans—Civil rights—
History—20th century. 2. Civil rights movements—History—20th century. 3. Race rela-
tions.] I. Title. II. Lucent library of historical eras. 1960s.
E185.615.U83 2004
323.1196'073—dc22
                                            2003020735

Printed in the United States of America

Contents

Foreword 4

Introduction: A Decade of Revolt
    Against Racism 6

Chapter 1: Preacher Power:
    Black Ministers Lead the Fight 10

Chapter 2: Sit-Ins:
    Young People Fight for Their Rights 22

Chapter 3: Freedom Riders:
    Integrating Interstate Travel 34

Chapter 4: Voter Registration:
    The Fight for the Right to Vote 46

Chapter 5: Black Power:
    A New Militancy for Blacks 58

Chapter 6: White Backlash:
    Resisting the Civil Righs Movement 72

Chapter 7: Black Pride:
    A New Mood Sweeps the Nation 84

Notes 95

For Further Reading 102

Works Consulted 103

Index 107

Picture Credits 112

About the Author 112

Foreword

Looking back from the vantage point of the present, history can be viewed as a myriad of intertwining roads paved by human events. Some paths stand out—broad highways whose mileposts, even from a distance of centuries, are clear. The events that propelled the rise to power of Germany's Third Reich, its role in World War II, and its eventual demise, for example, are well defined and documented.

Other roads are less distinct, their route sometimes hidden from view. Modern legislatures may have developed from old tribal councils, for example, but the links between them are indistinct in places, open to discussion and interpretation.

The architecture of civilization—law, religion, art, science, and government—as well as the more everyday aspects of our culture—what we eat, what we wear—all developed along the historical roads and byways. In that progression can be traced every facet of modern life.

A broad look back along these roads reveals that many paths—though of vastly different character—seem to converge at a few critical junctions. These intersections are those great historical eras that echo over the long, steady course of human history, extending beyond the past and into the present.

These epic periods of time are the focus of Lucent's Library of Historical Eras. They shine through the mists of history like beacons, illuminated by a burst of creativity that propels events forward—so bright that we, from thousands of years away, can clearly see the chain of events leading to the present.

Each Lucent Library of Historical Eras consists of a set of books that highlight various aspects of these major eras. For example, the Elizabethan England library features volumes on Queen Elizabeth I and her court, Elizabethan theater, the great playwrights, and everyday life in Elizabethan London.

The mini-library approach allows for the division of each era into its most significant and most interesting parts and the exploration of those parts in depth. Also, social and cultural trends as well as illustrative documents and eyewitness accounts can be prominently featured in individual volumes.

Lucent's Library of Historical Eras presents a wealth of information to young readers. The lively narrative, fully documented primary and secondary source quotations, maps, photographs, sidebars, and annotated bibliographies serve as launching points for class discussion and further research.

In studying the great historical eras, students also develop a better understanding of our own times. What we learn from the past and how we apply it in the present may shape the future and may determine whether our era will be a guiding light to those traveling future roads.

Introduction

A Decade of Revolt Against Racism

One of the most dramatic protests of the civil rights movement occurred on May 2, 1963, when six thousand young people ranging in age from six to sixteen marched through the streets of Birmingham, Alabama. They peacefully sang songs and waved to bystanders as they strolled from the Sixteenth Street Baptist Church to the city's segregated downtown area. There they calmly knelt in the street and prayed while the police arrested 959 boys and girls and jammed them into police vans bound for jail.

On May 8, Judge Talbott Ellis sternly lectured fifteen-year-old Grosbeck Preer Parham. Grosbeck had been charged with parading without a permit, but the real reason he and hundreds of other young people had been jailed was that they had dared to protest southern laws that denied blacks their rights because of the color of their skin. Instead of being intimidated by the judge, Grosbeck defiantly answered several of Ellis's questions before the judge finally released him from custody:

Ellis: Now, Grosbeck, you know violence in the streets is not the answer to this. I often think of what one of the founding fathers [of America] said: "There is no freedom without restraint." Now, I want you to go home and go back to school. Will you do that? [When Parham did not answer, the judge asked] Are you mad at me, son?

Grosbeck: Can I say something?

Ellis: Anything you like.

Grosbeck: Well, you can say that about freedom because you've got your freedom. The Constitution says we're all equal but Negroes aren't equal.

Ellis: But your people [blacks] have made gains and they still are. It takes time.

Grosbeck: We've been waiting over one hundred years.[1]

A Long Wait

The verbal exchange showed that, like many other southern whites, Ellis could not understand the profound change in attitude that was taking place in Grosbeck and other African Americans in the 1960s.

In that historic decade blacks made their greatest strides in securing their civil liberties. They were motivated by fury that a century after slavery had been abolished racist laws and attitudes still denied blacks many of their rights as U.S. citizens.

Segregation

When the decade of the sixties began, blacks in southern states were still segregated from whites. The color line between blacks and whites was strictly drawn by racist southern laws, which were collectively known as "Jim Crow"; the name came from a song performed in the 1830s by Daddy Rice, a white minstrel show entertainer who painted his face black when he performed. Jim Crow ruled almost every facet of daily life, including the restaurants blacks could eat at, the seats they could use in movie theaters and on buses, and the schools they could attend. Blacks who went to college had to attend all-black schools. Public facilities including toilets and drinking fountains were marked "White" or "Colored" to make sure people of both races knew which they could use.

The Reverend Ralph Abernathy, a Baptist minister from Montgomery, Alabama, once explained some of the indignities he and other blacks had to endure:

Even in the public courthouse, blacks could not drink water

except from the fountain labeled "Colored." You had a restroom for white males and a restroom for white women, and you had a restroom for colored. Meaning that colored people had to use the same restroom,

A man walks out of a waiting room for blacks at a Mississippi bus station. Before the civil rights movement, such segregated facilities were the norm in the South.

Rosa Parks was arrested in 1955 for refusing to surrender her seat on a Montgomery, Alabama, bus to a white man. In response, the city's black community organized a bus boycott.

male and female. And the janitor never would clean up the restroom for the colored people.[2]

In addition to such degrading daily humiliations, racist attitudes denied southern blacks a chance to hold all but the most menial jobs, robbed them of their right to vote, and forced them to act subserviently to whites out of fear that members of violent racist groups like the Ku Klux Klan (KKK) would beat or murder them for not being properly respectful to whites. Living conditions for blacks were better outside the South, where racism was not as overt or powerful. But even in big cities like New York, Detroit, Chicago, and Los Angeles, which all had large black populations, discrimination limited where they could live, attend school, and work.

The fight for civil rights that flowered in the 1960s was born from the anger, resentment, and frustration African Americans felt at the way they had been treated since the end of the Civil War. And this fight was sparked by an act of resistance by a black woman in Montgomery, Alabama, who was finally ready to stand up to racism.

Igniting the Civil Rights Fight

On December 1, 1955, Rosa Parks was riding a public bus home from a long, tiring day of work as a seamstress at the downtown Montgomery Fair Department Store. Alabama buses were segregated by law, with blacks being required to ride in the back. Even more humiliating, black men and women could be forced to give up their seats to whites if the vehicle became crowded.

Several stops after Parks had paid her dime for a seat, the bus driver ordered her to get up so a white man could sit down. Even though she knew she could be arrested and jailed for disobeying him, Parks refused. Years later, she explained why: "Just having paid for a seat and riding for only a couple of blocks and then having to stand was too much. There had to be a stopping place [for racist treatment], and this seemed to have been the place for me to stop being pushed around and to find out what human rights I had, if any."[3] The driver contacted the police, who arrested Parks. Her arrest ignited a 381-day boycott of the city bus system by hundreds of Montgomery blacks and a lawsuit that resulted in the U.S. Supreme Court overturning the Alabama law segregating buses. The historic boycott was led by a local pastor, Reverend Martin Luther King Jr., who would go on to become the greatest civil rights leader in America. As black power advocate Eldridge Cleaver would write a decade later in *Soul on Ice*, "somewhere in the universe, a gear in the machinery shifted"[4] when Parks took her brave stand against racism.

The gear that Parks moved marked the beginning of the civil rights movement, which flourished in the 1960s with sit-ins to protest segregated restaurants and other public places, Freedom Rides to break the color barrier on interstate bus travel, and a heroic effort to register blacks to vote so they could finally wield the political power needed to make their lives better. Thousands of men, women, and children, black and white, Christian and Jew, would put their lives on the line as Parks did to change the way blacks were treated in America.

White Resistance

To accomplish their difficult task, the crusaders who fought for civil rights in the 1960s risked being harassed, jailed, beaten, bombed, and even murdered because of the racist anger that met their efforts. This violence came at the hands of thousands of racists who wished to deny blacks their rights so blacks would remain powerless against whites.

But blacks no longer were willing to live that way. And throughout the 1960s, they fought for the justice and equality to which they were entitled as Americans.

Preacher Power: Black Ministers Lead the Fight

During the 1960s, black ministers were one of the most important groups that waged the battle for civil rights. In small southern communities and large northern cities, black churches became meeting places, rallying points, and organizational centers for the protests, demonstrations, and other activities that would topple the many forms of racism that confronted African Americans.

The ministers who headed those churches easily and naturally assumed leadership in the civil rights battles of this tumultuous decade. The Reverend Joseph E. Lowery, a Methodist from Mobile, Alabama, explains why they were uniquely qualified to guide the effort to achieve equality:

There are things in the black community that are not fully understood in the white community as it relates to the preacher. In the black community, historically, it has been the preacher who has been the principal community leader. Now there are several reasons for this. One was, of course, educational. He usually could read and write and had exposure to educational experiences that gave him some advantage. But beneath this was the fact that he was the freest leader in the community. The black congregation supported him [financially], so even though he did solicit a lotta support from the white community for various church causes, actually he was more independent than any other black person in the community.[5]

Even civil rights groups that had no religious affiliation, such as the Congress of Racial Equality (CORE), worked closely with ministers. Said Gordon Carey, a white CORE field secretary: "When we [went to southern cities] we went directly to the movement-oriented churches [because] that's where the protest activities were being planned and organized."[6]

The power of black preachers to lead the fight for civil rights in their communities became magnified in 1957 with the creation of the Southern Christian Leadership Conference (SCLC). Formed and led by black ministers throughout the South, SCLC became one of the most influential groups during the 1960s in helping blacks secure their rights. Lowery

Explaining Civil Rights in Biblical Terms

One of the strengths black preachers had was their ability to put events into biblical terms, which helped other blacks understand the importance and relevance of what was happening and made those incidents more dramatic. In 1961, when college students in Nashville, Tennessee, were arrested for trying to integrate local restaurants, the Reverend Kelly Miller Smith defended them in a sermon at First Baptist Church. He compared the students to Jesus Christ, who was arrested and put to death by Roman soldiers even though he was innocent of any crime. Smith's words are from To Redeem the Soul of America: The Southern Christian Leadership Conference and Martin Luther King, Jr. *by Adam Fairclough.*

The students sat at the lunch counters alone to eat and, when refused service, to wait and pray. And as they sat there on that southern Mount of Olives, the Roman soldiers, garbed in the uniforms of Nashville policemen and wielding night sticks, came and led the praying children away. As they walked down the streets, through a red light, and toward Golgotha, the segregationist mob shouted jeers, pushed and shoved them, and spat in their face, but the suffering students never said a mumbling word. Once the martyr mounts the Cross, wears the crown of thorns, and feels the pierce of the sword in his side there is no turning back. And there is no turning back for those who follow in the martyr's steps. All we can do is to hold fast to what we believe, suffer what we must suffer if we would win, and as we face our enemy let us say, "Father, forgive them, for they know not what they do."

believes the SCLC's religious base gave the group a moral force that could not be denied even by its enemies because many of them were also Christians:

> Because it had a preacher leadership it emphasized the moral aspects [of the fight for civil rights, which] were there before the political and legal aspects overshadowed them. But with the coming of SCLC, the struggle was put into its proper perspective in the moral arena, and that's what got people marching. It opened up people's eyes for the first time to how ugly and immoral segregation was.[7]

SCLC also became important because it was headed by the Reverend Martin Luther King Jr., a Baptist minister from Montgomery, Alabama. He was the most powerful and celebrated civil rights crusader in American history.

Martin Luther King Jr.

King was born into a family of ministers on January 15, 1929, in Atlanta, Georgia. His father, Martin Luther King Sr., was pastor of Ebenezer Baptist Church, which his maternal grandfather, Adam Daniel Williams, had also headed. The young boy who would grow up to lead the civil rights movement had a more secure and comfortable life than most blacks, but even the son

of the pastor of a notable black church was not exempt from racism. When King was eleven years old, a white woman in a department store slapped him, saying loudly for all to hear, "The little nigger stepped on my foot."[8] Although in that period "Negro" was the polite term for blacks, the woman felt free to use the most demeaning term and to strike the young boy. The hateful incident was neither the

Martin Luther King Jr. believed that nonviolent protest was the ideal means to achieve racial equality in the United States.

first nor the last King would endure while growing up, and he always resented such treatment: "I could never adjust to the separate waiting rooms, separate eating places, separate restrooms, partly because the separate [facility] was always unequal and partly because the very idea of separate did something to my sense of dignity and self respect."[9]

After graduating with a bachelor's degree in sociology from Morehouse College in Atlanta, King attended Crozer Theological Seminary in Chester, Pennsylvania, and then Boston University, where he earned a doctorate in theology in 1955. In Boston King met Coretta Scott, a native of Alabama who was studying voice at Boston's New England Conservatory of Music. They were married on June 18, 1953. It was not long after their marriage that they had to make one of the most important decisions of their lives.

Martin and Coretta had both enjoyed living in the North, where racism was not as prevalent and they were allowed more freedom than in the South. But they decided they should return to the South, where they believed blacks were finally ready to begin battling for the civil rights that had long been denied them there. "We came to the conclusion that we had the moral obligation to return, at least for a few years,"[10] King wrote years later.

On October 31, 1954, King was installed as the twentieth pastor of Dexter Avenue Baptist Church in Montgomery, Alabama's state capital. There he would emerge as the nation's most important black leader.

King Leads a Boycott

King's powerful leadership of the Montgomery bus boycott made him famous. But what impressed Americans the most, whether they were black or white, was King's insistence on nonviolence. He held true to this powerful philosophy even after a bomb exploded at his home on January 30, 1956, damaging the house but leaving Coretta and their infant daughter, Yolanda, unharmed. Even though some blacks suggested retaliating against the racist whites who had thrown the bomb, King told them to remain peaceful: "He who lives by the sword will perish by the sword. Remember, that is what God said. We are not advocating violence. We want to love our enemies. We must love our white brothers no matter what they do to us."[11] King's reliance on nonviolence and his insistence that racism was morally wrong would ignite peaceful protests in other southern cities. The nonviolent tactics King pioneered in Montgomery became the basis of civil rights battles for the next decade.

SCLC Is Born

The question confronting southern blacks after the Montgomery bus boycott was how to continue the new offensive against racism. At the invitation of King, the Reverend Charles K. Steele of Tallahassee, Florida, and the Reverend Fred L. Shuttlesworth of Birmingham, Alabama, ministers from eleven southern states met in Atlanta on January 10–11, 1957, to create the SCLC. Coretta King explains why it was important that SCLC was organized and led by black preachers:

> Most of the delegates were activist leaders of their southern black communities but more importantly to us, they were also ministers. Our organization was, from the first, church-oriented, both in its leadership and membership and in the ideal of nonviolence—a spiritual concept in deep accord with the American Negro's Christian beliefs.[12]

Although not every black minister who joined the fight for civil rights belonged to SCLC, it became the major organization for black preachers battling racism. SCLC was a loose confederation of scores of religious, civic, and civil rights groups, which paid only twenty-five dollars to become members. This central organization helped those groups plan and conduct programs to oppose segregation, register black voters, and fight discrimination in nonviolent ways. King was elected president, Steele first vice president, Shuttlesworth secretary, and the Reverend Ralph Abernathy of Montgomery treasurer.

King's fame suited him to represent SCLC to the world, and he spent much of his time traveling and giving speeches to raise funds and promote civil rights. While King brought in a lot of money, church members often funded their pastors' SCLC participation. According to Lowery,

> If we had a meeting [to attend], we'd ask our churches to pay our fare to the meeting. And if they didn't have it in the [church] treasury, they'd take up an offering. Admittedly, that probably has some advantages over other organizations that didn't have a lot of preachers who had a base from which they could draw resources to help them in the Movement.[13]

Individual pastors, with help from SCLC, fought racism in their own communities. In the 1960s, their efforts sparked some of the decade's fiercest, most successful, and sometimes bloodiest battles for equality.

Violence in Birmingham

In a CBS television story aired on March 13, 1961, reporter Howard K. Smith labeled Shuttlesworth, a Birmingham native and pastor of Bethel Baptist Church in Collegeville, "the man most feared by Southern racists [because of his bravery] and the voice of the new militancy among Birmingham Negroes."[14] Shuttlesworth had been fighting racism long before he joined SCLC. In 1956 he founded the Alabama Christian Movement for Human Rights (ACMHR), a powerful group that fought for black rights, and in the 1960s he continued to wage civil rights campaigns.

An empty bus moves along a Montgomery street during the boycott. Inspired by the boycott's success, King formed the Southern Christian Leadership Conference, an organization dedicated to fighting racism.

For his efforts, Shuttlesworth was beaten several times by racist whites, once with chains, and his home and church were both bombed. Nothing, however, could scare him. "I had the drive to get things done—an obsession, really, about overcoming segregation—and fear just didn't bother me,"[15] he once said. As Shuttlesworth had discovered, Birmingham was home to some of the South's most violent racists. It was also the scene of one of the bloodiest fights for civil rights, a series of protests in the spring of 1963.

Although Shuttlesworth in 1961 accepted an offer to head Revelation Baptist Church in Cincinnati, Ohio, he returned to Birmingham several times a month to fight racism there. On April 3, 1963, Shuttlesworth began a new round of protests by leading fifty-two people into five whites-only stores. He and nineteen other people were arrested and by April 10 more than three hundred people had been jailed on charges of parading without a permit. The most important arrest came on April 13, when King, at Shuttlesworth's invitation, joined the protests and was arrested. While in jail, King wrote his famous "Letter from Birmingham Jail," an eloquent, dramatic appeal against racism that was widely printed and made the Birmingham situation known worldwide.

In early May, local officials became so angered over the continued marches and demonstrations that they began reacting violently. They beat men, women, and children with clubs, released attack dogs that bit the marchers, and knocked them down with torrents of water from powerful hoses.

One of the injured protesters was Shuttlesworth. While leading marchers through city streets, he was recognized and a firefighter manning a hose said, "Hey, let's put some water on the reverend."[16] The high-pressure stream blast-ed Shuttlesworth off his feet and slammed him into a brick wall, breaking a rib and knocking him unconscious. Shuttlesworth later remembered that as the water struck him, he prayed, "Lord, I've been coming this way a long time. This is it. I'm ready when you are," but then heard a voice say, "Not here; not yet."[17]

After regaining consciousness, Shuttlesworth slowly got to his feet. Despite being battered and dazed, he immediately began marching again, convinced that his fight for civil rights must continue.

Reverend Fred Shuttlesworth meets with Birmingham activists to organize demonstrations against segregation.

Moral Authority

Shuttlesworth was one of many black ministers who were injured or physically assaulted while crusading against racism. Another was the Reverend C.T. (Cordy Tindell) Vivian, a Baptist minister of Selma, Alabama, and SCLC staff member. On February 16, 1963, Vivian led a small group of demonstrators to the county courthouse in Selma to protest a new policy that would slow the registration of black voters; the new procedure had been created because racist whites feared giving blacks political power.

At the courthouse, Vivian confronted Dallas County sheriff Jim Clark, who with several armed deputies was barring the door that led to the room where blacks could register. Vivian lectured the deputies, condemning their actions against blacks as morally wrong:

There are those who followed [German dictator Adolf] Hitler like you blindly follow this Sheriff Clark. You're racists in the same way Hitler was a racist. You can't keep anyone in the U.S. from voting without hurting the rights of all other citizens. Democracy's built on this. This is why every man has the right to vote. These people have the right to stand inside this courthouse. If you had your basic civics courses, you'd know this, gentlemen.[18]

Television cameras had recorded the speech, but Clark ordered journalists to turn their cameras off. After they did, Clark struck Vivian in the mouth, knocking him to the ground and bloodying his lip. When Vivian arose, he looked the sheriff in the eye and coolly said, "You can arrest us, Sheriff Clark. You don't have to beat us. You beat people bloody in order that they will not have the privilege to vote."[19]

The story of Clark's attack on Vivian became dramatic testimony of how bitter the fight for civil rights had become. Vivian's statements were widely reported on news shows that night. Lowery showed similar courage in April 1965 as the spokesperson for a group of blacks who met with Alabama governor George Wallace about the state's racial problems. Lowery remembers lecturing Wallace that day on racism:

We really challenged the governor that day on a moral basis. I wouldn't let him get in the political arena. I said to him that, "I am speaking to you as a Methodist preacher to a Methodist layman," which he is, and I said, "God has given you great gifts, great gifts of leadership, powers of persuasion, and he will call you to account for how you use them."[20]

The fact that so many black ministers fought for civil rights was important. It made many people, black and white, realize how morally wrong racism was from the viewpoint of the Christian religion that many people of the two races shared.

SCLC Staff Workers

Although many ministers such as Shuttlesworth and Lowery initiated protests against racism on their own, they often depended on SCLC for funds and other logistical help to make them successful. Thus SCLC workers, many of them ministers themselves, were also key participants in fighting racism.

In early 1960 the Reverend Wyatt Tee Walker, already involved in civil rights as pastor of a Baptist church in Petersburg, Virginia, became SCLC's executive director. In addition to administering the group's activities from its Atlanta headquarters and helping plan major protests, Walker accompanied King when he traveled: "My job was to book the airplane reservations, book us into the hotel, filter the calls, arrange the schedule of who we were going to see in the city, keep on time with the appointments."[21] Helping King was important because King's presence at protests did two important thing—it won additional news coverage and inspired the local residents. Accompanying King was the part of his work that Walker loved the most: "There wasn't anything I wouldn't do for Martin Luther King, because I sensed his commitment to that struggle and I respected leadership. I used to have to tell staff, 'Don't call Dr. King "Martin." He's our leader. You call him "Dr. King" around here.'"[22]

SCLC staff members played key roles in planning and running some of the decade's most dramatic events, historical incidents that would publicize racial injustice in America and around the world. For example, in March 1965 several hundred people marched from Selma to Montgomery, after several weeks of protests in Selma had been marred by white violence. The Reverend Andrew Young, an SCLC staffer, remembers that coordinating the marchers and the supplies they needed was a difficult task:

> The march from Selma to Montgomery, from my perspective, was a job. We had three hundred people to feed every day. We had to find a place to pitch tents, and we had to be concerned about security all along the road. There was absolutely nothing romantic about it. I was running back and forth trying to keep the march together and solving problems from one end to the other. I figure anytime they marched ten miles, I did closer to forty.[23]

Black and White

Although many black ministers like Young gladly worked for the cause of civil rights, not all joined the fight. Some black preachers disagreed with the new protest tactics, others thought that churches should not be involved in social issues or that blacks should go slower in seeking equality, and a few were afraid of retaliation by racist whites. One preacher who did not back the civil rights movement was the Reverend Percy Green, pastor of Easter Star Baptist Church in Demopolis, Alabama. In March 1965, when blacks began boycotting white businesses there in an effort to end segregation, Green made a radio broadcast to persuade blacks to stop:

> My friends, whenever we bring political structure into the House of God or use it [at church] to teach youth and adults to group themselves together and stand in front of our business establishments and forbid our people to go in and buy what they desire [then] you have left the teachings of Jesus Christ out of the church and Christ is not pleased with it.[24]

Green was accused of siding with whites because he was a store owner himself. However, when local blacks started boycotting his store and members of his own congregation complained to him about his position, he began supporting the protests.

Yet most black ministers fought whole-heartedly for civil rights. And they were sometimes joined by white religious leaders like the Reverend Joseph Ellwanger, leader of the Concerned White Citizens of Alabama. On March 6, 1963, during the Birmingham protests, Ellwanger read a passionate statement condemning racism. On the steps of the Dallas County courthouse, the spot where Sheriff Clark had knocked C.T. Vivian to the ground only a few weeks earlier, Ellwanger said that he and other whites had

come to Selma today to tell the nation that there are white people in Alabama who will speak out against the events which have recently occurred [in Selma and other Alabama communities]. We are horrified at the brutal

Reverend Wyatt Tee Walker's Dangerous Night

Like most leaders of the civil rights movement, the Reverend Wyatt Tee Walker, the SCLC's executive director, believed deeply in nonviolence. But on May 21, 1963, his faith in that concept was tested after the Gaston Hotel in Birmingham, Alabama, was bombed because it was the headquarters for SCLC staff members coordinating protests in that city against racism. In fact, Walker's life was probably saved that night by a reporter who kept him from resorting to violence after a state trooper struck his wife, Ann, with a rifle, splitting her head open and sending her to the hospital. Walker explained the incident in Voices of Freedom: An Oral History of the Civil Rights Movement from the 1950s Through the 1980s *by Henry Hampton and Steve Fayer.*

I was [at the scene of the incident] within a matter of moments. A UPI [United Press International] reporter from Mississippi, Bob Gordon, who was a segregationist up to this time, saved my life, because I asked him which state trooper had hit my wife. He pointed him out, and I started for him. Then Gordon [realizing Walker could be hurt by the trooper] tackled me and threw me to the floor and held me down. Then it occurred to me that this guy would take this automatic rifle and shoot me as quickly as he had brained my wife. Well, if Bob Gordon had not wrestled me to the floor, I think aside from me probably losing my life or being seriously maimed or injured, it would have done irreparable harm to the nonviolent movement. However, I just wasn't thinking about anything except that my wife had been injured with the carbine and that was the man who did it.

way in which the police at times have attempted to break up peaceful assemblies and demonstrations by American citizens who are exercising their constitutional right to protest injustice.[25]

As always, the fact that the message was coming from a minister, no matter what his skin color, gave the words deeper meaning for those who heard them.

Preacher Power in Action

The power black preachers exerted in their communities was never more clear-ly shown than in Birmingham, the site of one of the decade's most violent and bitter protests. Andrew Young explains how church leaders not only became leaders in the civil rights battle but enlisted members of their congregations for the cause:

We often talk about the "hand of God" in the leadership. There were four young men in Birmingham, in churches, that had come there within a year, that happened to be pastors of the largest churches in the city. John Cross at 16th Street Baptist

Church leaders Andrew Young (left) and Martin Luther King Jr. (right) were influential figures in the fight for civil rights. In addition to serving as leaders of the movement, they enlisted many supporters from their congregations.

King Writes a Letter

One of the most eloquent appeals against racism ever written was penned by the Reverend Martin Luther King Jr. after his arrest in Birmingham, Alabama, on April 10, 1963, for violating a court order barring demonstrations against segregation. In his "Letter from Birmingham Jail," which he wrote while confined in a cell, King explained to the world why blacks were now willing to risk imprisonment for freedom. The letter was an answer to eight white Birmingham ministers who had publicly criticized the protests for being "unwise and untimely." Excerpts from King's letter are from the Creighton University website.

I am in Birmingham because injustice is here. . . . We know through painful experience that freedom is never voluntarily given by the oppressor; it must be demanded by the oppressed. For years now I have heard the word "Wait!" It rings in the ear of every Negro with piercing familiarity. This "Wait" has almost always meant "Never." We must come to see, with one of our distinguished jurists, that "justice too long delayed is justice denied."

Church, A.D. King [Martin Luther King Jr.'s brother] had just gone to First Baptist, Nelson Smith at New Pilgrim, and John Porter at Sixth Avenue Baptist. The members of those four Baptist Churches gave the movement a constituency of five-thousand—to start with. When you add that constituency to the 500 or 600 that Fred Shuttlesworth had organized, we had the basis of a movement.[26]

Sit-Ins: Young People Fight for Their Rights

On February 1, 1960, four black students from North Carolina Agricultural and Technical College—Ezell Blair Jr., Franklin McCain, David Richmond, and Joseph McNeil—sat down at the lunch counter at the F.W. Woolworth Company store in Greensboro, North Carolina. When Blair asked for a cup of coffee, the response from the white waitress was one he had expected: "We don't serve colored in here."[27] McCain then reminded her that the students had already bought toothpaste and several other items in the store. "I beg your pardon," McCain said. "You just served me at a counter two feet away [for those purchases]. Why is it that you serve me at one counter and deny me at another?"[28]

When the waitress still refused to serve them, the students did something unexpected—they continued to sit quietly for more than thirty minutes until the store closed at 5:30 P.M., when they left. Accompanied by twenty more students, they returned the next day to ask politely for a cup of coffee, and they kept coming back day after day with the same simple request. Each time that the students were ignored, they opened textbooks and studied. As time went on, they were joined by other black college and high school students, even a few whites.

The four eighteen-year-old freshmen did not know it, but they had just launched the sit-in phase of the civil rights movement, a new form of peaceful protest that quickly spread across the South. In the next year seventy thousand people, most of them college and high school students, staged sit-ins in more than a hundred southern cities. Although thirty-six hundred people were arrested in such protests, their valiant efforts began to topple the barriers of segregation that had always made blacks second-class citizens in their own hometowns.

Sit-Ins Spread

The students had decided to challenge segregation during late-night talks in their college dormitory. "Four guys met, planned, and went into action," McCain said. "It's as simple as that."[29] As their target they chose the local Woolworth five-and-dime store, where most items cost a nickel or dime, because blacks were allowed to shop at Woolworth but not dine there.

They were not, however, the first to use the sit-in tactic. Between 1943 and 1960, similar protests had taken place in at least sixteen cities, including Chicago, Illinois; St. Louis, Missouri; Baltimore, Maryland; and Nashville, Tennessee. Those earlier sit-ins never gained much attention from the news media or support from other blacks.

This time, however, the tactic, like a forest fire sparked by one tiny flame, captured the imagination of young blacks. College students who believed it was time to challenge segregation started sit-ins in

Four black college students stage a sit-in at a Greensboro, North Carolina, lunch counter. The young men were the first to practice sit-ins as a form of peaceful protest against segregation.

other southern communities. Within a week sit-ins had begun in a half-dozen other North Carolina communities, and within two weeks similar protests were under-way in fifteen cities in five southern states.

On February 13, black students in Nashville launched their first full-scale sit-ins at Kress, Woolworth, and McClellan stores. Nashville became a dynamic protest center because of strong leaders like James Lawson, a thirty-one-year-old divinity school student at Vanderbilt University. Lawson believes the sit-ins succeeded in 1960 after failing earlier because of one man—the Reverend Martin Luther King Jr. Lawson argues that King's success in integrating buses in Montgomery, Alabama, and his dependence on nonviolence as a tactic inspired young people. Said Lawson, "King had emerged and was ready and was preaching and teaching

Planning to Fight Racism

The decision to stage the sit-in against segregation at Woolworth in Greensboro, North Carolina, was made informally by four North Carolina Agricultural and Technical College freshmen. In My Soul Is Rested: Movement Days in the Deep South Remembered *by Howell Raines, Franklin McCain explains how he and Ezell Blair Jr., David Richmond, and Joseph McNeil made their historic decision.*

The planning process was on a Sunday night, I remember it quite well. I think it was Joseph who said, "It's time we take some action now." After selecting the technique, then we said, "Let's go down and ask for service." It certainly wasn't titled a "sit-in" or "sit-down" at that time. Let's just go down to Woolworth's tomorrow and ask for service and the tactic is going to be simply this: we'll just stay there. We never anticipated being served, certainly, the first day anyway. We'll stay until we get served. And I think Ezell said, "Well, you know that might be weeks, that might be months, that might be never." And I think it was the consensus of the group, we said, "Well, that's just the chance we'll have to take." What's likely to happen? Now, I think that was a question that all of us asked ourselves. What's going to happen once we sit down? Of course, nobody had the answers. Even your wildest imagination couldn't lead you to believe what would, in fact, happen [that they would ignite a chain of similar protests].

direct action, nonviolent action and was clearly ready to act, ready to seed any movement that needed sustenance and growth. In other words the soil had been prepared."[30]

SNCC Is Formed

The burning desire for change that King had helped instill in young people enabled the sit-in movement to spread rapidly, with many college and high school students taking the initiative to organize protests. Cordell Reagon explains how he and other students at his high school in Nashville decided to stage a sit-in: "Oh, we went to the lunch room, we went from table to table and some people talked it up in their classes through whispering and everything. And when time came [to protest], we just knocked on doors and said it was time."[31]

In addition, ministers affiliated with the Southern Christian Leadership Conference (SCLC), like the Reverend Kelly Miller Smith in Nashville, helped organize some sit-ins. One of the key people in advancing the sit-in movement was Ella Baker, a longtime civil rights activist who was SCLC's executive director. Excited by the new protests, Baker called people she knew at various colleges, asking, "What are you all going to do? It is time to move."[32]

Baker, the granddaughter of a rebellious slave minister, realized the importance of the protests. Because she believed students needed to band together to make sure the sit-ins continued, Baker persuaded SCLC to sponsor a conference at Shaw University in Raleigh, North Carolina. More than two hundred students attended the meeting, which went from April 15 to 17, 1960. The meeting resulted in the formation of the Student Nonviolent Coordinating Committee (SNCC). SNCC—its initials were pronounced "snick" by friend and foe alike—would become a major force in the fight for civil rights throughout the 1960s by organizing sit-ins, registering voters, and participating in other activities.

King delivered the keynote speech to the students. But their mood was eloquently described in a powerful talk by Lawson, who had been expelled from Vanderbilt because of his sit-in activities just three months before he was to receive his bachelor of divinity degree. In his remarks, Lawson declared:

These are exciting moments in which to live. Reflect how over the last few weeks, the "sit-in" movement has leaped from campus to campus, until today hardly any campus remains unaffected. At the beginning of this decade, the student generation was "silent," "uncommitted" [but] after only four months, these analogies largely used by adults appear as hasty clichés which should not have been used in the first place. [The protests show] that American students were simply waiting in suspension; waiting for that cause, that ideal, that event which would catapult their right to speak powerfully to their nation and world.[33]

Training in Nonviolence

One of the greatest contributions King had made to setting the stage for sit-ins was to show that nonviolent protest could defeat racism. Even before the sit-ins began, the SCLC was teaching blacks how to protest peacefully. Like King, Lawson had gone to India to study the nonviolent tactics which Mohandas Gandhi had used in the 1940s to win India's freedom from Great Britain. And groups like the Fellowship of Reconciliation (FOR) and Congress for Racial Equality (CORE) had stressed nonviolence for several decades.

After the first sit-ins began, however, even more people needed training in nonviolence. Classes were held in many communities, including Nashville, which had a slew of volunteers from its four black colleges—Fisk University, Tennessee State College, American Baptist Theological Seminary, and Meharry Medical School.

One of the important things sit-in leaders tried to teach the volunteers was why the protests would so greatly anger local residents. Jane Stembridge, a white student at Union Theological College in Atlanta, told volunteers that the whites they met would consider the protests a personal attack against them and the way they lived. She explained that a black person sitting down at a white lunch counter "is a collision between this one person and that person."[34]

Because white anger often ignited violence against protesters, training sometimes included dramatizations in which students posing as racists would curse or hit fellow demonstrators to prepare them to deal with such situations. Protesters were taught how to protect themselves and remain nonviolent while being arrested by police or harassed and attacked by belligerent whites. Before blacks from Claflin College and South Carolina State University went to a Kress lunch counter on February 25, 1960, in Orangeburg, South Carolina, they learned the following guidelines:

> You may choose to face physical assault without protecting yourself, hands at the sides, unclenched; or you may choose to protect yourself, making plain [to police or attackers] you do not intend to hit back. If you choose to protect yourself, you practice positions such as these:
>
> To protect the skull, fold hands over the head.
>
> To prevent disfigurement of the face, bring the elbows together in front of the eyes.
>
> For girls, to prevent internal injury from kicks, lie on the side and bring the knees upward to the chin; for boys, kneel down and arch over, with skull and face protected.[35]

But even after receiving such training, many demonstrators were still not sure how they would react if someone hit them. Bernard Lafayette, a student at American Baptist Theological Seminary in Nashville, wondered how he would respond:

I was curious to know how I would feel if I were struck physically for standing up for what I believed was right. I was more concerned about what was happening on the inside of me—what my reaction would be. How would I feel about that person? Could I, in fact, find a place in my heart to love someone, not to hate someone, who was physically abusing me?[36]

Although Lafayette was in fact hit during demonstrations, he always remained nonviolent. He said he was able to do so because, "You see, they [white racists] were afraid. I was not."[37]

Sitting Down for Justice

Many sit-ins, however, were free of violence. On February 13, when students at Florida Agricultural and Mining College in Tallahassee, Florida, went to a Woolworth, Patricia Stephens remembers that white patrons ignored them. "The regular customers," she said, "continued to eat. When one man finished, the waitress said: 'Thank you for staying and eating in all this indecency.' The man replied: 'What did you expect me to do? I paid for it.'"[38]

Mississippi activists continue their sit-in despite being attacked and harassed by onlookers. Sit-in protesters were trained to remain nonviolent even in the face of aggression.

And when the sit-ins began in Nashville on February 12, Diane Nash said workers in the targeted Woolworth were more fearful than the students. "The first sit-in we had was really funny," said Nash. "The waitresses were nervous. They must have dropped $2,000 worth of dishes that day. It was almost like a cartoon." [39]

Nash was a Chicago, Illinois, native who had never experienced segregation until she attended Fisk University. She became active in fighting racism after she went to the Tennessee State Fair and was stunned to see, for the first time, bathroom signs that read "WHITE WOMEN" and "COLORED WOMEN." The segregation seemed so demeaning to Nash that she vowed to fight against it.

But when the sit-in protests began, even committed leaders like Nash had to learn to control their fear about what might happen to them. Once, when Nash was going from store to store to check on the progress of sit-ins, she was recognized while making her way through a crowd of angry whites:

I heard one young guy in a group of teenagers say, "That's Diane Nash. She was in the paper. She's the one to get." And I realized somebody could stab me or something and not even be seen. I got terrified. And so I made a deal with myself. I'd take five minutes during which I'd make a decision that I was going to either put the fear out of my mind and do what I had to do, or I was going to call off the sit-in and resign. I really just couldn't function effectively, as afraid as I was. And I found the courage to put the fear out of my mind and keep functioning. [40]

Many other protesters found that same sort of bravery in themselves. In a 1961 sit-in in Atlanta, Georgia, Stembridge sat next to Lana Taylor, a black student from Spelman College. Stembridge was amazed by Taylor's courage when the store manager tried to bully her:

The manager walked up behind her, said something obscene, and grabbed her by the shoulders. "Get the hell out of here." Lana was not going. I did not know [then] she should have collapsed in a nonviolent manner [according to training]. She probably did not know. She put her hands under the counter and held. He was rough and strong. She just held and I looked down at that moment at her hands . . . every muscle holding. All of a sudden he let go and left. I thought he knew he would not move that girl—ever. [41]

Protesters also tried to integrate other public facilities. In Jackson, Mississippi, nine Tougaloo College students were arrested on March 27, 1961, when they tried to check books out of the main branch of the Jackson Public Library. The main branch had more of the books they needed for their schoolwork than the library branch that blacks had to use.

Although the protesters failed to integrate the library, their attempt received a lot of news media coverage. Protester James Bradford remembers that several journalists who had been alerted to the event were on hand to witness what happened: "When we got out of the cars the media was there. They popped out of the bushes or wherever they had been hiding and the cameras started to roll."[42] The reporters, who dubbed the students the "Tougaloo Nine," accompanied them to jail. Arrested on charges of breach of the peace for trying to check out a book, the students were held for thirty-two hours. The charges were later dismissed. The following day, when other students marched to the jail to support them, police dispersed the crowd with clubs, tear gas, and police dogs.

White Violence

Although initial protests were usually calm affairs, the longer they went on, the angrier whites became—and that anger often fueled hateful acts against sit-in participants. Candie Anderson, a white attending Fisk University, remembers how whites bothered Nashville demonstrators:

Young kids threw French fried potatoes at us, and gum, and cigarette butts. I looked down the counter at Barbara Crosby, in a straight pink skirt and nice white blouse, and at Stephen in a dark suit, with a calcu-

lus book. The policemen simply lined up behind us and peeled us two by two off the stools. The crowd in the store shouted out approval.[43]

Anderson, because she was white, received special attention from the crowd, with people yelling insults and taunting her for supporting blacks. "My stomach always hurt a little on the way to a sit-in," she admitted years later. "I guess it's the [fear of the] unexpected."[44]

Edward Rodman, who was a high school student in Portsmouth, Virginia, remembers there was no trouble when he and other students sat at a lunch counter at Rose's Variety Store on February 12, 1960. But four days later at another store, he and the other protesters were confronted by a group of white youths who instigated a fight:

Outside [one] boy stood in the middle of the street daring any Negro to cross a certain line. . . . When we did not respond, he became so infuriated that he struck a Negro boy in the face with [a] chain. The boy kept walking. Then, in utter frustration, the white boy picked up a street sign and threw it at a Negro girl. It hit her and the fight began. The white boys, armed with chains, pipes, and a hammer, cut off any escape through the streets. Negro boys grabbed the chains and beat the white boys. The hammer they threw away. The white boys went running back to their hot rods.[45]

A Disciple of Nonviolence

The nonviolent philosophy the Reverend Martin Luther King Jr. adopted to win the Montgomery, Alabama, fight for integrated seating on public buses became the powerful foundation for sit-ins and other civil rights activities. In Stride Toward Freedom: The Montgomery Story, *King explains this concept.*

From the beginning, a basic philosophy guided the Movement. This guiding principle has since been referred to variously as nonviolent resistance, noncooperation, and passive resistance. But in the first days of the protest none of these expressions was mentioned; the phrase most often heard was "Christian love." It was the Sermon on the Mount, rather than a doctrine of passive resistance, that initially inspired the Negroes of Montgomery to dignified social action. It was Jesus of Nazareth that stirred the Negroes to protest with the creative weapon of love. As the days unfolded, the inspiration of Mahatma Gandhi began to exert its influence. I had come to see early that the Christian doctrine of love operating through the Gandhian method of nonviolence was one of the most potent weapons available to the Negro in his struggle for freedom. About a week after the protest started, a white woman who understood and sympathized with the Negroes' effort wrote a letter to the editor of the *Montgomery Advertiser* comparing the bus protest with the Gandhian effort in India. [Not long after that]

people who had never heard of the little brown saint of India were now saying his name with an air of familiarity. Nonviolent resistance had emerged as the technique of the movement, while love stood as the regulating ideal. In other words, Christ furnished the spirit and motivation, while Gandhi furnished the method.

Mahatma Gandhi influenced King's belief in the importance of nonviolent protest.

Although whites lost this battle, they won many others. On April 14, 1961, blacks in Biloxi, Mississippi, tried a different form of protest—a "wade-in" at a beach on the Gulf of Mexico. But when Dr. Gilbert Mason and a few friends tried to swim, police told them they were not allowed to use any of the twenty-six-mile stretch of sandy beaches. Ten days later, when Mason led another group back there, a mob of forty white men assaulted them with iron pipes, chains, and baseball bats while police officers stood and watched. When Mason tried to go back onto the beach to assist a friend who had been beaten unconscious, a policeman stopped him, saying, "Get off this beach before I blow your brains out."[46]

Although most southern whites opposed integration, some had mixed feelings about unruly whites. Even though the *Richmond News Leader* objected to integration, the newspaper ran an editorial in its February 2, 1960, issue that commented unfavorably on rowdy Richmond youths who had harassed sit-in protesters. The editorial claimed that "many a Virginian must have felt a tinge of wry regret" because of the stark contrast between the appearance of the two groups:

Here were the colored students, in coats, white shirts, ties, and one of them was reading Goethe [a German author] and one was taking notes from a biology text. And on the sidewalk outside was a gang of white boys come to heckle, a rag-tail rabble, slack-jawed, black-jacketed, grinning fit to kill, and some of them, God save the mark, were waving the proud and honored flag of the Southern States in the last war fought by gentlemen [the Civil War]. Eheu! It gives one pause.[47]

The Sit-Ins Succeed

The students were determined to defeat segregation, but it was not easy. In Greensboro it took six months of protests and negotiations with local business owners and public officials before whites consented to end segregation of lunch counters and some other public facilities, such as toilets and drinking fountains. In other southern cities and towns, it would take years for white leaders to end segregation.

Success, however, came quickly in Nashville. On May 10, 1960, Nashville became the first major southern city to begin desegregating public facilities. That victory, however, came only after a violent incident that frightened both whites and blacks alike. On April 19, the home of Z. Alexander Looby, a Trinidad-born black attorney who represented students arrested in the sit-ins, was heavily damaged by a bomb. The dynamite blast was so strong that it blew out 147 windows in nearby Meharry Medical School. The racist act spurred a march on City Hall by two thousand blacks in which Diane Nash, the Fisk University student who helped lead the sit-ins, challenged Mayor Ben West by asking him directly if he believed racism

A Jew Joins the Protests

In April 1960, Henry Schwarzchild and his wife, Kathy, were driving home to Chicago, Illinois, when he decided to participate in a lunch counter protest in Lexington, Kentucky. For Schwarzchild, a Jew born in Germany who served in the U.S. Army in World War II, it was an easy decision. His family had fled to America in 1939 after Adolf Hitler came to power. Schwarzchild knew all about prejudice—Hitler had killed 6 million Jews. Schwarzchild had never been able to understand how most German citizens could stand by and do nothing to stop the killing. In Free at Last: The Civil Rights Movement and the People Who Made It *by Fred Powledge, Schwarzchild explains why he joined the sit-ins.*

The one thing that I concluded [about the failure of German citizens to stop Jewish deaths] was that I would not want to say to myself at the end of my life that when there were enormously significant things going on in my society, I did nothing. The one unforgivable sin would be to stand by and let them happen and do nothing. It seemed to me that the civil rights movement was, after the experience of Hitler and the Holocaust, sort of the closest to that that was liable to come down the pike. I remember being there for a couple of hours, marching up and down the street with a bunch of black folks from Lexington, and we didn't even, as I remember it, enter the store and we were certainly not in that sense technically a sit-in. It was more a sympathy demonstration with the sit-ins. And there were no arrests while I was part of that group.

Schwharzchild, however, would be arrested in later demonstrations. After returning to Chicago, he joined the Congress of Racial Equality and continued to participate in the civil rights movement in the South.

was morally right. "I confronted Mayor West with what his feelings were as a man, as a person,"[48] Nash said. The mayor's response surprised Nash and many other people in Nashville and around the nation. Years later, West remembered how he felt when Nash questioned him:

They [marchers] asked me some pretty soul-searching questions. And one that was addressed to me as a man. And I found that I had to answer it frankly and honestly—that I did not agree that it was morally right for someone to sell them merchandise and refuse them service. And I had to answer it just exactly like that. It was a moral question—one that a *man* had to answer, not a politician.[49]

Soon the walls of segregation began to crumble in other cities. In less than twenty months from January 1960 to August 1961, the sit-ins led to integration of restaurants, toilets, drinking fountains, and some other public facilities in more than one hundred cities and towns in southern and border states.

The victories marked an important new phase in the fight for black civil rights. The sit-ins were the first successful protests since the bus boycotts in the South that were sparked by the effort in Montgomery in 1955. However, the changes the sit-ins enacted were limited—segregation still held sway in Deep South states like Alabama and Mississippi, where blacks dared not sit down at a Woolworth lunch counter for fear of being beaten, and there were pockets of segregation in many other southern states. It would take many more protests, as well as federal legislation,

throughout the decade to destroy Jim Crow and give blacks all the rights they deserved as citizens.

It Tasted the Same

Blacks who lived in communities where sit-ins had won them their rights were now able to learn what Leo Lillard, a Tennessee State University student who participated in the Nashville sit-ins, had discovered as a youngster. Lillard once reminisced about an incident when he was growing up that had taught him something about segregation:

When I was a boy, Nashville was a divided town. One day [my mother and I] were at Kress's, [which] had these beautiful marble water fountains. One said "Colored" and one said "White." I went over to both fountains and tasted the water and told my mother, "Tastes the same to me, Mom."[50]

Now, southern blacks in many communities could learn the same thing.

Chapter

3

Freedom Riders: Integrating Interstate Travel

On May 26, 1961, Howard University student William Mahoney boarded a Greyhound bus that left Washington, D.C., for Montgomery, Alabama. At the vehicle's first stop in Virginia, Mahoney was confronted with the segregation that not only separated the races but condemned blacks to inferior bathrooms, restaurants, and other public facilities. Mahoney wrote of what he discovered:

I [saw] what the Southern white has called "separate but equal." A modern rest station with gleaming [lunch] counter and picture windows was labeled "White," and a small wooden shack beside it was tagged "Colored." The colored waiting room was filthy, in need of repair, and overcrowded. When we entered the white waiting room Frank [Hunt, a fellow Freedom Rider] was promptly but courteously, in the Southern manner, asked to leave. Because I am a fair-skinned Negro I was [mistakenly] waited upon. I walked back to the bus through the cool night trembling and perspiring.[51]

Even though Mahoney and other passengers on the bus were protected by National Guardsmen armed in battle gear, he was frightened because he had just broken the South's racial barrier by using white facilities. Mahoney had good reason to be fearful. He was a Freedom Rider, one of hundreds of white and black men and women who rode buses into the South in 1961 to challenge the racism that still existed even after the U.S. Supreme Court had outlawed segregation of interstate bus stations. Many of the Freedom Riders before Mahoney, as well as those who would come afterward, had been beaten bloody, sometimes with chains and pipes, and thrown into jail for their efforts.

The 1961 Freedom Rides lasted only a few months. But the bravery Freedom Riders showed by challenging racism would carve out a glorious chapter in the fight for civil rights.

Testing the Law

The Freedom Riders of 1961 were not the first who challenged segregated interstate bus travel. In 1947 black and white volunteers sponsored by the Congress of Racial Equality (CORE) and the Fellowship of Reconciliation (FOR), two northern civil rights groups, rode buses for two weeks through segregated states like Virginia, North Carolina, Tennessee, and Kentucky. Those ancestors of the Freedom Riders, who called their trip a "Journey of Reconciliation," sat together on buses and used both colored and white public facilities such as bathrooms.

James Peck, a forty-six-year-old white who was a rider in both 1947 and 1961, notes, however, that the early attempt at integration did not venture into the Deep South, states like Alabama and Mississippi where segregation was stricter and racists

more violent. In his 1962 book *Freedom Ride*, Peck wrote about the first attempt of blacks and whites to ride buses together:

> To penetrate the Deep South at that time [the forties] would simply have meant immediate arrest of all participants, an end to the trip—and possibly of us. As a Negro told us on the first lap, "Some bus drivers are crazy; and the farther south you go, the crazier they get." Putting it still more

A Freedom Rider bleeds after being attacked by pro-segregationists at an Alabama bus station.

graphically, a white South Carolinian commented about one of our Negroes sitting in front, "In my state he would either move or be killed."[52]

The original experiment failed to accomplish any real change. But on February 1, 1961, James Farmer became national director of CORE, which he had helped found in 1942. He and other CORE members revived this dramatic method to challenge racism. They wanted to test a December 1960 Supreme Court decision that banned segregation in interstate travel facilities.

CORE decided to stage a "Freedom Ride" in which volunteers would travel into the South on buses operated by Greyhound and Trailways, national companies that had their own bus stations in most communities. On the bus the whites would sit in back and the blacks in front, the reverse of southern segregation, and in the bus terminals the blacks would use facilities in white waiting areas. "Our intention," Farmer said, "was to provoke the southern authorities into arresting us and thereby prodding the [U.S.] Justice Department into enforcing the law of the land [integration]."[53]

Getting Ready

CORE chose thirteen volunteers, seven blacks and six whites, for the first Freedom Ride. But before those first buses left Washington, D.C., on May 4, bound for New Orleans, Louisiana, the riders received training in how to handle difficult situations and whites who would react violently to their integration effort. Farmer

James Farmer, director of the Congress of Racial Equality, staged Freedom Rides in order to test a 1960 Supreme Court ruling that outlawed segregation in interstate travel.

describes how riders rehearsed being subjected to abuse they might receive:

We had some of the group of thirteen sit at a simulated counter asking for coffee. Somebody else refused them service, and then we'd have others come in as white hoodlums to [pretend to] beat 'em up and knock them off the counter and club 'em around and kick 'em in the ribs and stomp 'em, and they were quite realistic. [And] then we'd go into a discussion as to how the roles were played, whether there was something that the Freedom Riders did that they shouldn't have done, said that they shouldn't have said. Then we'd reverse roles and play it over and over again and have lengthy discussions of it.[54]

Farmer also wrote to President John F. Kennedy, Attorney General Robert F. Kennedy, and other federal officials about the protest, so that if trouble arose they could provide protection for the riders. Farmer never received a reply, but the Kennedys were aware of the situation and monitored the ride's progress. Peck and Farmer, the first two volunteers, were joined by college students, many of them, like John Lewis of Nashville, Tennessee, veterans of the 1960 sit-ins. Because some people left and others joined the traveling protest as it wound its way south, more than the original thirteen volunteers participated in the initial Freedom Ride.

Because the buses were headed into the Deep South, where racists still fiercely opposed integration, riders knew violence was likely. Lewis remembers that the night before the bus left, the group ate together. "To me," Lewis said later, "this meal was like the Last Supper, because you didn't know what to expect going on the Freedom Ride."[55]

The Ride Begins

On May 4, the riders split into two groups to depart Washington on separate Greyhound and Trailways buses. Their route was supposed to carry them through North and South Carolina, Georgia, Alabama, and Mississippi before ending in New Orleans on May 17. The end date was chosen because it was the seventh anniversary of *Brown v. Board of Education*, the 1954 U.S. Supreme Court decision that declared segregated schools illegal but had done little to integrate black and white students throughout the nation since then.

The initial stops the buses made were routine, with no problems even though the Freedom Riders were integrating rest stops. Peck recalls the first time his bus pulled into a bus station: "The first white and colored signs encountered were only fifty miles south of Washington—atop the restroom doors at the Greyhound stop in Fredericksburg [Virginia]. Charles Person, a Negro student from Atlanta, went into the white rest room and I went into the colored rest room without incident."[56] The first arrest occurred on May 8 in

Freedom Riders board a bus during their historic May 1961 ride. When the activists arrived in Anniston, Alabama, an angry mob of pro-segregationists attacked them.

Charlotte, North Carolina. James Perkins was arrested for trespassing for trying to get his shoes shined in the white area; he was acquitted of the charge the next day and resumed his journey. Violence, however, came on May 9 when Lewis and Albert Bigelow, a retired white navy officer, were knocked to the ground by two whites as they neared the white waiting room in a Greyhound station in Rock Hill, South Carolina. After police intervened, the two men were allowed to enter the white area.

The Freedom Riders continued their journey despite several other minor incidents and a Justice Department warning that there might be violence in Birmingham, Alabama. Trouble struck even before they got to that city.

Violence Strikes

At the Greyhound station in Anniston, Alabama, riders were greeted by a hostile mob that included members of the Ku Klux Klan (KKK), a violent racist group. Because the whites were armed with pistols, clubs, chains, and knives, the riders stayed on the bus. However, before the vehicle left the terminal, the racists slashed its tires. When the tires went flat about six miles outside the city, the bus was surrounded by about a hundred people who had followed in cars.

Although the whites were prevented from entering the bus by Ell Cowling, an Alabama state trooper who had accompanied the riders to provide protection, someone threw a firebomb into the bus, setting it ablaze. Hank Thomas, a black college student, remembers how frightening it was when the whites would not let them leave the burning bus:

They closed the doors and wouldn't let us off. But then I'm pretty sure they realized that [the bus might explode] and so they started scattering, and I guess that's the way we got off the bus. . . . That's the only time I was really, really afraid. I got whacked over the head with a rock or I think some kind of a stick as I was coming off the bus.[57]

When the riders did get off, some of them were beaten. They were then taken to a hospital and treated for smoke inhalation and other injuries. Unable to continue the trip by bus, the riders contacted the Reverend Fred Shuttlesworth, secretary of the Southern Christian Leadership Conference (SCLC), who formed a car

Arrested for Trying Buy a Ticket

Some of the Freedom Riders were arrested even before they got on a bus. On November 22, 1961, Bertha Gober was one of five Albany State College students arrested just for trying to buy a ticket from the white terminal at a bus station in Albany, Georgia. In addition to being arrested, she was also suspended from college. Gober's account of the arrest is from A Documentary History of the Negro People in the United States 1960–1968, *edited by Herbert Aptheker.*

I went to the ticket window. I stood directly behind a white man that was purchasing his ticket. I stood there for five seconds when this uniformed officer said: "You'll never get your ticket there." I asked why. Still no answer. Then [a police detective] came up and introduced himself and said my appearance there "was tending to create a disturbance." He gave me a choice of going to the Negro waiting room or to be arrested. I informed him that I would not leave until I had purchased my ticket. He took me outside where [Police Chief Laurie] Pritchett was waiting. We then went to the [police] station. I felt that as a human being not of Albany but of the United States of America that I had a right to use all facilities. I felt it was necessary to show the people that human dignity must be obtained even if through suffering or mistreatment. I'd do it again anytime. After spending those two nights in jail for a worthy cause, I feel I have gained a feeling of decency and self-respect, a feeling of cleanliness that even the dirtiest walls of Albany jail nor the actions of my institution cannot take away from me.

caravan to transport them to Birmingham.

When the Trailways bus pulled into Anniston a little later, eight whites forced their way on board, beat one black and two white riders, and forced the riders to the back of the bus. They then rode with the Freedom Riders to Birmingham where angry whites, full of hate and armed with sticks and other weapons, were lined up on the sidewalk outside the bus station. Despite the racist mob, James Peck and Charles Person got off the bus and entered the white waiting room. Peck explains what happened then:

> We were grabbed bodily and pushed toward the alleyway leading to the loading platform. As soon as we got into the alleyway and out of sight of onlookers in the waiting room, six of them started swinging at me with fists and pipes. Five others attacked another person a few feet ahead. Within seconds, I was unconscious on the ground.[58]

Peck required fifty-three stitches to close his head wounds; other riders, as well as some reporters and photographers, were also beaten. The whites attacked without any interference from police, who were mysteriously absent. Public Safety Commissioner Bull Connor later claimed that he did not have enough officers to send.

New Riders

On May 15, both bus companies refused to drive the riders any farther because they feared their buses would be wrecked. The riders, many of them injured, decided to fly to New Orleans because they felt they had made their point about racism.

This valiant protest might have ended in Birmingham if it had not been for Diane Nash, who had helped lead the sit-ins in Nashville, Tennessee. Nash was now a leader of the Student Nonviolent Coordinating Committee (SNCC) and an employee of the Nashville Christian Leadership Conference (NCLC), which was affiliated with the SCLC. She telephoned Shuttlesworth and said she could enlist students to continue the ride. "Young lady, do you know that the Freedom Riders were almost killed here?" asked Shuttlesworth, to which Nash replied, "Yes, and this is exactly why the ride must not be stopped."[59] Shuttlesworth, impressed with her bravery, promptly agreed.

Nash, bewildered and angered by the segregation she encountered in Nashville, claimed the ride had to continue because, "if the Freedom Riders had been stopped as a result of violence, I strongly believe that the future of the movement was going to be cut short. The impression would have been that whenever a movement starts, all [racists need to do] is attack it with massive violence and the blacks will stop."[60] Nash recruited two dozen students who joined three original riders—Farmer, Lewis, and Thomas—in Birmingham; the Freedom Ride had now become a joint project of CORE, SCLC, and SNCC, three of the period's most powerful civil rights groups.

With its tires slashed, the Freedom Riders bus was forced to stop just outside Anniston. Angry whites then burned the bus and beat many of its passengers.

On May 20, the riders boarded two Greyhound buses for Montgomery after federal officials persuaded the Greyhound and Trailways companies to serve the passengers. No trouble was expected because Alabama governor John Patterson had promised to protect travelers after meeting with U.S. Justice Department official John Seigenthaler, who now followed the buses in a rented car.

During the trip, a state plane flew overhead and state patrol cars accompanied the buses. But in Montgomery, the protective plane and cars disappeared, and at the bus terminal, riders were greeted by several hundred armed, angry whites. Explains Lewis: "People came out of nowhere—men, women, children, with baseball bats, clubs, chains—and there was

no police official around. They just started beating people."[61]

The first rider off the bus was James Zwerg, a white University of Wisconsin student. Encouraged by the women in the crowd, more than a dozen males beat Zwerg to the ground and kicked him in the head, leaving him unconscious. Frederick Leonard, a black Freedom Rider, believes that Zwerg's bravery may have protected Leonard and other blacks: "He had a lot of nerve. And I think what saved me, Bernard Lafayette and Allen Kasen [was that] Zwerg walked off the bus in front of us, and it was like they were possessed—they couldn't believe there was a white man who would help us. And they grabbed him and pulled him into the mob."[62] There were no police to stop the racist rampage even though the Federal Bureau of Investigation had notified Police Commissioner L.B. Sullivan to protect the riders. The bus terminal became a nightmare scene of blood and boiling hatred. Rider Ruby Doris Smith describes what she saw: "They started beating everyone. I saw John Lewis beaten, blood coming out of his mouth. People were running from all over. Every one of the fellows was hit. Some of them tried to take refuge in the post office, but they were turned out."[63] More than a half-dozen riders as well as bystanders, both black and white, were beaten severely enough to require medical attention. Among them was Seigenthaler, who arrived while the attack was going on and was knocked unconscious while trying to help two women escape the savage mob.

End Point—Jackson, Mississippi

The violence shocked the nation and angered President Kennedy, who ordered six hundred federal marshals to protect the riders. A rally to support the Freedom Riders, featuring the Reverend Martin Luther King Jr., was held the next night at First Baptist Church. Its pastor was King's good friend, the Reverend David Abernathy.

As darkness descended, the church became ringed by several thousand angry whites, who set cars on fire and shot guns into the air. With only a thin line of federal marshals to protect those inside the church, including the riders, King told over fifteen hundred people, "The law may not be able to make a man love me, but it can keep him from lynching me."[64]

When the whites refused to disperse, trapping those in the church, King telephoned Attorney General Kennedy, who then contacted Governor Patterson. Kennedy persuaded the governor to declare martial law by activating the Alabama National Guard. The soldiers finally arrived about 3 A.M. to disperse the hateful crowd so people who had spent the entire night in the church could leave.

The violence, however, did not stop the Freedom Riders from leaving on May 24 for Jackson, Mississippi. Two Trailways buses were protected by an escort of Alabama National Guardsmen until they crossed into Mississippi, where guardsmen from that state took over. When the buses arrived in Jackson, there were no hostile crowds; the Freedom Riders got off and went to the white terminal. It was then that the ride came to an abrupt halt—police arrested Farmer and twenty-six other riders on charges of trespassing, breach of the peace, and refusal to obey an officer. Frederick Leonard explains how police effectively ended the ride, something racist thugs had failed to do: "As we walked through [the terminal], the police just said, 'Keep moving' and let us go through to the white side. We never got stopped. They just said, 'Keep moving,' and they passed us right on through the white terminal into the paddy wagon and into jail. There was no violence in Mississippi."[65]

Among those taken into custody was the Reverend C.T. Vivian, although he

A Federal Official Is Struck Down

One of the victims of the attack on Freedom Riders in Montgomery, Alabama, on May 20, 1961, was John Seigenthaler, a U.S. Justice Department official whom President Kennedy had dispatched to monitor the situation. Driving a rented car to follow the bus, Seigenthaler arrived in Montgomery while the riders were being attacked. In Eyes on the Prize: America's Civil Rights Years, 1954–1965 *by Juan Williams, Seigenthaler explains how he was attacked.*

The Freedom Riders emerging from the bus were being mauled. It looked like two hundred, three hundred people all over them. There were screams and shouts. As I drove along I saw two young women being pummeled by a woman who was walking behind one of these young women. She had a purse on a strap and was beating [one woman] over the head and a young, skinny blond teenager in a T-shirt was sort of dancing backwards in front of her [the Freedom Rider], punching her in the face. I bumped the car onto the sidewalk, blew the horn, jumped out of the car, grabbed the one who was being hit, took her back to the car. The other Freedom Rider got into the car. If she [the first rider] had gotten into the car, I think I could have gotten away. But [a] moment of hesitation gave the mob a chance to collect their wits, and one [person] grabbed me by the arm, wheeled me around and said, "What the hell are you doing?" I said, "Get back! I'm a federal man." I turned back to the Freedom Rider, and the light went out. I [was] hit with a pipe over one ear. I literally don't remember anything that happened [after that].

Federal marshals patrol a Montgomery street to protect the Freedom Riders.

almost evaded capture because he had gone directly to the bathroom. When Vivian came back into the terminal and saw what was happening, he went up to a deputy sheriff and bravely announced, "I'm with them. [It was] probably the only time someone asked [the sheriff] to be arrested."[66]

Jail and Prison

A day after Mississippi authorities had thrown all the protesters in jail, a trial was held. Leonard claims the quick trial was a racist sham: "While [attorney Jack Young] was defending us, the judge turned his back, looked at the wall. When he finished, the judge turned around—bam, sixty days [in jail]."[67]

Despite the threat of more jail sentences, the Freedom Rides continued through the summer, with hundreds of people making such journeys, including an interfaith group of Jewish and Christian religious leaders. Over three hundred peo-

Waiting in Birmingham

After the second batch of volunteers arrived in Birmingham, Alabama, in May 1961 to continue the Freedom Ride, they had to wait several days for one of the bus companies to provide a vehicle. As a result, the Freedom Riders wound up spending the night of May 19–20 at the Birmingham bus station. The overnight stay was tense because members of the racist Ku Klux Klan, most wearing robes, were also there to try to intimidate them. Bernard Lafayette, a black college student, explains the experience in this excerpt from Free at Last: The Civil Rights Movement and the People Who Made It *by Fred Powledge.*

We stayed there overnight. I remember that we all went to the rest room in a group because no one wanted to be caught in the rest room alone. We couldn't use the white rest room because it was in the white side of the bus station. We started toward the [black] rest room, and these whites, the Klan members and such, would surge forward. We didn't know what to expect out of the policemen [on hand to protect them], because they didn't stop the Klan from coming around and stepping on our feet and throwing ice water on us when we were asleep. So we all went together to the rest room. There were so many of us. The Klan rose up, and then the policemen did. They didn't want a conflict inside the rest room, so they stopped the Klan from going in. Some of the policemen, I imagine, also were Klan members, but they just had different uniforms on at the time.

ple were arrested in Jackson, Mississippi, and taken to the Hinds County Jail. Howard University student William Mahoney, who was arrested May 28 on a charge of breach of peace, described the conditions as terrible:

The thirty or more of us [arrested] occupied five cells and a dining hall on the top floor. At night we slept on lumpy bags of cotton and were locked in small, dirty, blood-spattered, roach-infested cells. Days were passed in the hot, overcrowded dining room, playing cards, reading, praying. Time crawled painfully [and] the killing of a roach or the taking of a shower became major events. The jailers' initial hostility was broken down by responding to it with respect and with good humor.[68]

Police, however, rarely treated their prisoners with respect. When Vivian was arrested, officers kept hitting him during questioning because he refused to add "sir" when answering them. "I was beaten more than anybody else," Vivian admitted.[69]

But riders like Vivian and Mahoney were soon sent to an even more terrible place—Parchman Prison, one of the toughest and worst southern prisons. Mississippi officials transferred the protesters to state prisons because local jails were overflowing with Freedom Riders and to intimidate future protesters, a tactic that failed to work. In addition to bad food, dirty cells, and damp, cold conditions, the guards were frightening. Stokely Carmichael, a SNCC member who would later head that group, said guards called him demeaning names and tried to scare him: "I'll never forget this [one guard]— he used to wear those big boots. He'd say, 'Why you always trying to be so uppity for? I'm going to see to it that you don't ever get out of this place.'"[70]

Victory

Although some riders served sentences as long as six months, most were out in forty days. In the end, their sacrifices resulted in victory. Although the Supreme Court had declared such segregation illegal, the federal government had not enacted any regulations to enforce the ruling. But President Kennedy on May 29, 1961, ordered the Interstate Commerce Commission (ICC) to issue a regulation banning segregation in interstate bus terminals. The ICC issued the order on September 22 and it became effective on November 1.

The bravery Freedom Riders showed by enduring racial hatred, physical assaults, and grim jail sentences made them heroes. The pride they had in what they did is embodied in this stanza from a 1960s folk song:

Yes, we are the Freedom Riders,
And we ride a long Greyhound;
White or black,
we know no difference,
Lord, for we are Glory bound.[71]

Voter Registration: The Fight for the Right to Vote

In 1961 the Reverend June Dowdy, pastor of two black churches in Fayette County, Tennessee, went to Somerville to register to vote. After being ignored several times when he asked where he could sign up, the minister finally got an answer, although not one that would do him much good: "I asked one white man where the registration office was and he directed me to go down to Hatchie Bottom. That's the swamp along the Hatchie River, where a Negro was lynched back about 1940 after he tried to vote."[72] It seems inconceivable today that citizens would be threatened with death for trying to exercise their constitutional right to vote. But in the early 1960s the fear of violent reprisals by racist whites and com-

plicated, illegal procedures which made it almost impossible for southern blacks to register kept all but a few of them from becoming voters. Between 1952 and 1960 in Fayette County, for example, only seventeen blacks cast ballots in elections.

In 1961 the civil rights movement began to concentrate on ensuring southern blacks this important right. Sit-ins and Freedom Rides had achieved moderate gains against segregation, but blacks knew they would never achieve true equality until they had political power to elect officials, black or white, who would not discriminate against them. The Reverend Martin Luther King Jr. once said, "Give us the ballot and we will no longer have to worry the federal government about our basic rights. We will no longer plead—we will write the proper laws on the books. Give us the ballot, and we will fill the legislatures with men of good will."[73]

The drive to register black voters became one of the most difficult and violent phases of the civil rights fight. Whites denied blacks this important right to keep them powerless. Whites were deathly afraid of black voters because they outnumbered whites in many southern areas, as in Fayette County, where blacks in 1961 made up 68.5 percent of the population. This fear was explained to a *New York Times* reporter by a white man from Fayette County: "Sure I reckon it's all right for a [black] to vote if he wants to and it don't harm nothing, but what if they all begun to vote here! We'd [whites] be swamped. You put yourself in our place and you'll see why we got to keep them in their place."[74]

To overcome such mindless racism, black and white workers for groups like the Student Nonviolent Coordinating Committee (SNCC), Southern Christian Leadership Conference (SCLC), and Congress of Racial Equality (CORE) flooded the South in the early 1960s. Together with local residents, they would help blacks gain the one right they needed the most to improve their lives—the right to vote.

Police officers attack protesters of race discrimination in voter registration. Attempts to register black voters led to some of the most violent clashes of the civil rights movement.

Moses and Moore

The first SNCC registration campaign was begun in McComb, Mississippi, in 1961 by Robert Moses, a Harvard University graduate who would become a legendary civil rights figure. In the summer of 1960, while on vacation from his job as a high school teacher in New York, Moses went to Atlanta, Georgia, to help in the fight for black rights. Moses became so committed to the cause that he quit teaching to work as a SNCC field secretary.

That first summer Moses met Amzie Moore, head of the Cleveland, Mississippi, branch of the National Association for the Advancement of Colored People (NAACP). Their subsequent friendship led to a drive to register voters in Mississippi, one of the most heavily segregated, racist states. Moore was impressed immediately with Moses:

> I knew Bob was a graduate from Harvard. I felt like if a man was educated, there wasn't very much you could tell him. I didn't think you could give him any advice. Bob was altogether different. Bob believed me and was willing to work with me. When I found out he was honestly seeking to help, then, in any way I could, I was willing to help him.[75]

Moses was equally taken with Moore, who had fought in a segregated unit of the armed forces during World War II and was now battling racism at home. Moore told Moses that only 5 percent of eligible black voters in Mississippi had been allowed to register and that in some of the state's eighty-three counties there were no black voters. Moore convinced Moses that voter registration was the most important black issue and that SNCC should become involved:

> Amzie laid out what was to become the voter registration project for the Delta [the rural area around the Mississippi River] of Mississippi. He wanted SNCC to come in and do it. I think he saw in the students what had been lacking—that is, some kind of deep commitment that no matter what the cost, people were going to get this done.[76]

SNCC Arrives

Moses and more than a dozen volunteers, many of them Freedom Riders recently released from jail, arrived in McComb, Mississippi, in July 1961 to begin registering voters. Other groups had attempted this in the past, but until Moses took over no one had ever succeeded.

The first task confronting Moses, as it would other organizers, was to gain the trust and respect of local black residents who would have to be brave enough to register. Moses did this by going from door to door to introduce himself, explain SNCC's plan, and recruit volunteers. "For two weeks," Moses said, "I did nothing but drive around the town talking to the business leaders, the ministers, the people in the town, asking them if they would support [the effort]."[77]

A Sheriff Tries to Intimidate Blacks

Southern law enforcement officials often tried to intimidate blacks who wanted to vote. During a voter registration rally on July 26, 1962, at Mount Olive Baptist Church in Sasser, Georgia, a meeting of thirty-eight blacks was interrupted by Terrell County sheriff Z.T. Mathews. He and two other officers, guns on their hips, glared at the would-be voters and two SNCC field-workers also present—Charles Sherrod, who was black, and Ralph Allen, a white. New York Times *reporter Claude Sitton wrote a story that captured the confrontation. The following excerpts from his article are from* Portrait of a Decade: The Second American Revolution *by Anthony Lewis and The* New York Times. *At one point, Mathews tried to get the blacks to admit that they did not think there was anything wrong with the way they were treated in his county.*

"I just want to find out how many here in Terrell County are dissatisfied. . . . Are any of you disturbed?" [Mathews] asked.

The reply was a muffled "Yes."

"Can you vote if you are qualified?"

"No."

"Do you need people to come down and tell you what to do?"

"Yes."

"Haven't you been getting along well for a hundred years?"

"No."

Sitton's portrayal of the meeting clearly shows that Mathews did not understand how angry Terrell County blacks were at the way they were treated, but it did make clear his own viewpoint: "We want our colored people to go on living like they have for the last hundred years."

When SNCC workers Cordell Reagon and Charles Sherrod arrived in Albany, Georgia, in the fall of 1961, their method was slightly different. Because they were college students, they focused on meeting young blacks. Reagon explains how they did this:

We slept in abandoned cars [because the students had little funding], and eventually we started going out on the college campus [Albany State University]. We would sit in the student union building on the college campus all day long, drinking soda, talking with the students, trying to convince them to [fight segregation]. [Eventually] we became a part of that community. And after people got over their initial fears of us [as strangers], I mean we were taken in as sons of the community. I mean, it got to the point where people didn't see us as being [from] out of town.[78]

The bonds between newcomers and black residents became close, but most whites were hostile to the SNCC members. Anne Moody, a Tougaloo (Mississippi) College student who volunteered for SNCC in 1964, said, "Those SNCC workers had friends everywhere. Among the Negroes, that is. The whites were just waiting to kill them off."[79] Their friendship with blacks was helpful. Because SNCC staffers were paid only $10 a week, and then only when SNCC had money, local blacks often fed and housed them.

Recruiting Voters

Enlisting new voters was not easy because many blacks worried that whites would retaliate against them. They not only feared loss of jobs or housing—some blacks who lived and worked on plantations were fired and evicted from their homes when they registered—but also dreaded violence by racist whites. Dorothy Cotton worked with the SCLC to prepare citizens to register. She said part of her task was getting them to lose their fear of whites and of the courthouses:

The courthouses was synonymous with the place where black folk got beat up and just abused, you know. And so at the end of hearing all of the problems [they would encounter] in the teaching session where you're really trying to turn people on to thinking new ways about themselves and their own functioning, we started to ask questions like, "Why aren't you [allowed to be] that clerk!" It blew their minds.[80]

Once people did volunteer, organizers had to teach them how to pass literacy tests that southern states had begun requiring in the 1950s to keep blacks from voting. The exams, which included questions on government, had always been a stumbling block for blacks because so many of them had little or no schooling. Complicating matters, in most states, registrants had to interpret a section of the state constitution. In 1955, when Mississippi passed such a law, a state legislator remarked, "if I wasn't already registered, I don't believe I could qualify to vote myself."[81]

Lawrence Guyot, who worked for SNCC in his home state of Mississippi, said registrars gave easy questions to whites and difficult ones to blacks. "Needless to say," Guyot said, "we had some Phi Beta Kappas [college honor students], some college and high school principals failing the literacy test."[82]

Organizers set up classes to teach people how to pass the tests, and sometimes even how to read and write so they could fill out the voting form. Once they had mastered how to register, they were ready for the greatest ordeal—signing up to vote.

Registering Voters

On August 15, Moses went to Liberty, Mississippi, in Amite County to register two women and one man. White officials, angry that blacks wanted to register, stalled them by dragging out the simple process for hours, a tactic other communities later used to make it hard for blacks to register. Moses explains,

> We arrived at the courthouse about 10 o'clock. The registrar came out. He asked them: "What did they want?" They didn't say anything. They were literally paralyzed with fear. I told him who I was [and] that they wanted an opportunity to register. Our people started to register, one at a time. In the meantime, a procession of people began moving in and out to the registration office: the sheriff, a couple of his deputies, people from the far office, the people who do the drivers' licenses—looking in, staring, moving back out, muttering. Finally finished the whole process about 4:30; all three of the people had a chance to register—at least to fill out the form. This was a victory.[83]

But whites who ruled Mississippi were angered by even such a small victory as the three blacks had achieved. While Moses was driving them home, a highway patrol officer stopped the car. Moses knew there would be trouble when the officer asked if he was the one "trying to register our niggers"[84] and began quizzing the blacks. When Moses asked what was going on, the patrol officer arrested him for interfering with an officer in the discharge of his duties. Moses was fined fifty dollars and spent two days in jail.

Jail time was minor compared to the violence Moses and other civil rights workers soon faced. When Moses returned on August 29 to register three more people, he was savagely beaten by Billy Jack Caston, a cousin of the county sheriff. Moses needed eight stitches to close a head wound, but Caston was never charged. On September 25, Herbert Lee, a black farmer who had helped people register, was murdered by F.H. Hurst, a white state legislator. Hurst claimed self-defense even though black witnesses said he pulled a gun and shot Lee for no reason. Hurst was never charged.

The slaying brought a new sense of responsibility to Moses and other workers: "Now we knew in our hearts and minds that Hurst was attacking Lee because of the voter registration drive, and I supposed that we all felt guilty and felt responsible."[85] The slaying frightened them, but it did not stop them from registering voters or stop blacks from being willing to register.

Fannie Lou Hamer

Moses once explained how important it was to recruit strong local residents for voter registration. "The quality of the person, the local person, that you work with is everything in terms of whether the project can get off the ground,"[86] he said. One of the local people on whom Moses came to depend was Fannie Lou Hamer, who with her husband lived and worked on a plantation in Ruleville in Sunflower County, Mississippi. When Hamer attended a registration meeting Moses held, she immediately wanted to vote:

Well, I didn't know anything about voting; I didn't know anything about registering to vote. One night I went to the church. They had a mass meeting. And I went to the church, and they talked about how it was our right, that we could register and vote. They were talking about we could vote out people that we didn't want in office, we thought that wasn't right, that we could vote them out. That sounded interesting enough to me that I wanted to try it. I had never heard, until 1962, that black people could register and vote.[87]

On August 31, 1962, Hamer registered in Indianola. When she returned to the plantation, the owner told her she had to withdraw her registration or be fired:

So I said, "Mr. Dee, I didn't go down there to register for you. I went down there to register for myself." And that made him madder, you know. [He then told her] "You got 'till in the mornin' to tell me. But if you don't go back there and withdraw, you got to leave the plantation."[88]

Because Hamer refused, she was kicked off the plantation where she had lived and worked for eighteen years. Hamer soon began helping other blacks register as a worker for SNCC and the Council of Federated Organizations (COFO), a coalition of Mississippi civil rights groups. Hamer became famous when she testified on national television at the 1964 Democratic National Convention about her experience registering voters, including a savage beating she received in a Mississippi jail in 1962 because of those efforts.

Freedom Summer

Voter registration drives in the early 1960s showed positive results, with the black vote increasing by as much as 50 percent or more. In Texas the black electorate jumped from 111,014 in 1962 to 375,000 in 1964, and in the same period Georgia and Florida both gained about 100,000 voters. And once they successfuly registered, the new black voters usually met no violence trying to vote because federal officials were on hand at polling places to prevent altercations.

But by 1964 there were only five thousand new voters in Mississippi, an increase of just 5 percent. Because racist opposition there was so deep-seated and violent, civil rights groups decided a special effort was needed. Called "Freedom Summer,"

Fannie Lou Hamer Is Beaten

It is hard to imagine how brutal some southern law enforcement officers could be when they dealt with blacks who wanted to vote. One of the most dramatic incidents involved Fannie Lou Hamer, who, after she registered to vote, began working to help other blacks gain the right to vote. In the summer of 1963, Hamer was arrested with six other blacks in the central Mississippi community of Winona for trying to eat at a white restaurant. When she was taken to jail, officials, angry over her voter registration activities, had her beaten by two black inmates. Hamer's account is from My Soul Is Rested: Movement Days in the Deep South Remembered *by Howell Raines.*

Well, the white folks here knowed I had tried to register, so they was goin' give me as much trouble as possible, 'cause when they come back [one of the men said], "You, bitch, you, we goin' make you wish you was dead." And let me tell you, before they stopped beatin' me, I wish they would have hit me one lick that could have ended the misery that they had me in. They had me to lay down on this bunk bed with my face down, and they had two black prisoners. You know, a lot of folks would say, "Well, I woulda died before I'd done that." But nobody knows the condition that those prisoners was in, before they were s'posed to beat me. And I heard that highway patrolman tell that black man, "If you don't beat her, you *know* what we'll do to you." And he didn't have no other choice. So they had me lay down on my face, and they beat with a thick leather thing that was wide. . . . And then after the first one beat, they ordered the second one to beat me, and when the second one started beatin', it was just—it was just too much.

Fannie Lou Hamer was severely beaten for helping blacks to register for the vote.

it was planned by Moses and Dave Dennis, CORE's Mississippi field director. Freedom Summer in 1964 would involve over eight hundred college students, three-fourths of them white. Dennis explains why so many whites were recruited: "The idea was to get the country to begin to respond to what was going on there. They were not gonna respond to a thousand blacks [but] would respond to a thousand young white college students."[89]

That tactic worked—the news media reported heavily about young whites heading south to fight racism. Although the whites found themselves immersed in a lifestyle they had never before experienced, they quickly made friends with the people they had come to help. Unita Blackwell, a resident of Sunflower County, Mississippi, who welcomed students, explains how they came together in harmony:

> There was interaction of blacks and whites. I remember cooking some pinto beans—that's all we had—and everybody just got around the pot, you know, and that was an experience just to see white people coming around the pot and getting a bowl and putting some stuff in it and then sitting around talking [and] laughing. I guess they became very real and very human, we each to one another.[90]

In the South, however, it was not normal for blacks and whites to socialize or even ride together in a car. Joanne Grant remembers that she and other whites had to take precautions when they traveled with blacks to avoid being harassed by racists: "When we drove around, if there were a large number of black people in the car, then the white people rode on the floor, and if there were a larger number of white people in the car, then the black people rode on the floor."[91] That type of precaution may sound silly today but racist violence was a reality. By the end of Freedom Summer, COFO reported more than 450 violent incidents—eighty citizens and voter registration workers were beaten, three wounded by gunfire in over thirty shootings, thirty-five churches burned, and thirty homes and buildings bombed. There had also been three deaths—brutal slayings that occurred at the start of the historic voter drive.

Murder in Mississippi

On June 20, 1963, the first students left for Mississippi from Oxford, Ohio, where they had received training on how to do their jobs. Just one day later, three civil rights workers were reported missing—Andrew Goodman, a twenty-year-old Queens (New York) College student; Michael Schwerner, a twenty-four-year-old white man who, with his wife, Rita, had established the CORE office in Meridian, Mississippi; and CORE worker James Chaney, a twenty-four-year-old black Mississippian. On June 21, on their way to investigate a church burning, they had been arrested for speeding near Philadelphia, Mississippi, by Neshoba County deputy sheriff Cecil Price. They

ANDREW GOODMAN   JAMES EARL CHANEY   MICHAEL HENRY SCHWERNER

On their way to investigate a church burning in Mississippi, civil rights activists Andrew Goodman, James Chaney, and Michael Schwerner were brutally murdered.

were released from jail that night. It was later determined that Price stopped their car a few miles away from the jail and turned them over to a group of whites, who killed them and buried their bodies at a dam construction site.

Rita Schwerner, who had been training volunteers in Oxford, went to Neshoba County with SNCC's Robert Zellner to find out what happened. In an angry confrontation with Sheriff Lawrence Rainey, she demanded to see her husband's car. When Rainey refused, Schwerner, despite the presence of angry whites surrounding them, defiantly told him, "I'm not leaving here until I learn what happened to my husband. I'm going to keep drawing attention here until I find out, and if you don't like it you'll just have to have me killed too."[92]

Federal authorities investigated the slayings. In August they arrested twenty whites, including Rainey and Price, and charged them with conspiracy to deprive the dead men of their civil rights. Federal officials did not seek to try them for murder in state courts because they knew white juries would find them innocent. In 1967 seven men were finally convicted, but Rainey and Price were found innocent.

Victory at Last

Although hundreds of people risked their lives during Freedom Summer, it resulted in the registration of only twelve hundred black voters. However, sensational media coverage of the brutal white retaliation against blacks who wanted only to vote angered people across the country. It also increased pressure on President Lyndon B. Johnson and Congress to pass legislation to ensure that blacks could vote.

Many other events served as catalysts for voter registration, including initially peaceful protests that descended into violence in the spring of 1965 in Selma, Alabama. The effort was led by King, who declared on January 2 in Selma's Brown Chapel [Methodist] Church, "We must be ready to go to jail by the thousands. We will bring a voting bill into being on the streets of Selma!"[93] Thousands of people were arrested during protests that

Herbert Lee's Murder

A farmer with nine children, Herbert Lee was shot to death in Amite County, Mississippi, on September 31, 1961, because he was helping people register to vote. Lee was shot by F.H. Hurst, a state legislator who was never charged because he claimed that he shot Lee in self-defense while Lee was bringing cotton to market. Civil rights worker Robert Moses, however, discovered the facts, which showed it had been a cold-blooded murder. His explanation of what witnesses told him is from The Eyes on the Prize Civil Rights Reader, *edited by Clayborne Carson and others.*

[They saw] Herbert Lee drive up in his truck with a load of cotton, F. Hurst following behind him in an empty truck. Hurst got out of his truck and came to the cab on the driver's side of Lee's truck and began arguing with Lee. [Hurst] pulled out a gun which he had under his shirt and began threatening Lee with it. One of the people that was close by said that Hurst was telling Lee, "I'm not fooling around this time, I really mean business," and that Lee told him, "Put the gun down. I won't talk to you unless you put the gun down." Hurst put the gun back under his coat and then Lee slid out on the other side, on the offside of the cab. As he got out, Hurst ran around the front of the cab, took his gun out again, pointed it at Lee and shot him. Hurst was acquitted. He never spent a moment in jail. I remember reading very bitterly in the papers the next morning [that a] Negro had been shot in self-defense as he was trying to attack F.H. Hurst. That was it. You might have thought he had been a bum.

extended into March, with television cameras and newspaper headlines capturing the violence that police and whites directed against demonstrators.

As King predicted, the Selma protests resulted in a voting bill. Johnson was so angered by the brutality there that on March 15 he addressed the nation to announce he would submit a voting rights bill to Congress. "All Americans," he declared, "should be indignant when one American is denied the right to vote. The loss of that right to a single citizen undermines the freedom of every citizen."[94]

Despite southern opposition, Congress passed the 1965 Voting Rights Act and Johnson signed it into law on August 6. The bill, for the first time, authorized federal intervention to make sure blacks could freely register and vote. In Mississippi alone, the number of black voters skyrocketed in just a few months from 33,000 to 150,000. By 1970 there were an estimated 3.5 million southern black voters. And their ballots tipped the balance of political power as they elected some seven hundred black sheriffs, mayors, council members, and state legislators in that one year alone.

Real Victors

In 1964, when Hamer participated in her first election, she voted for herself in a Democratic primary against Representative Jamie Whitten. "The first vote I cast, I cast for myself, because I was running for Congress,"[95] Hamer said proudly. She lost, but just being on the ballot had been a victory.

Although it was federal legislation that finally gave men and women like Hamer the right to vote, the bill became a reality due to the heroic work of thousands of people who fought for years to register voters. After Herbert Lee was killed in Mississipi, Albany State College student Bertha Gober wrote a song called "We'll Never Turn Back." This stanza from that famous song is a fitting tribute to Lee and everyone else who worked to help blacks vote:

We have walked through
the shadows of death,
We've had to walk all by ourselves.
We have hung our head and cried
For those like Lee who died,
Died for you and died for me,
Died for the cause of equality.[96]

Chapter 5

Black Power: A New Militancy for Blacks

Many historians believe that the single most important event in the civil rights movement occurred on August 28, 1963, when the March on Washington drew more than 250,000 people to the nation's capital. In the largest public protest Americans had ever witnessed, tens of thousands of people, black and white, old and young, jammed the grassy, open space between the Washington Monument and the Capitol in a dramatic show of support for black rights. It was a hot, sunny day, and while the thousands of people listened to music and speeches for hours, many dangled their feet in the Mall's giant reflecting pool.

Of all the speeches heard that day, the most stirring was by the Reverend Martin Luther King Jr. In words that will be remembered forever, King reduced the goal of the civil rights movement to a simple wish that all people, no matter what their color, could understand:

> I have a dream that my four little children will one day live in a nation where they will not be judged by the color of their skin, but the content of their character. [And] that day when all of God's children, black men and white men, Jews and Gentiles, Protestants and Catholics, will be able to join hands and sing in the words of the old Negro spiritual, "Free at last! Free at last! Thank God Almighty, we are free at last!"[97]

Not all blacks, however, gloried in the day's events. A dissenter was Malcolm X, the fiery, intellectual spokesman for the Nation of Islam. Malcolm would later comment derisively:

Yes, I was there. I observed that circus. Who ever heard of angry revolutionists all harmonizing "We Shall Overcome . . . Some Day . . . " while tripping and swarming along arm-in-arm with the very people they were supposed to be angrily revolting against? Who ever heard of angry revolutionists swinging their bare feet together with their oppressor in lily pad park pools, with gospels and guitars and "I Have A Dream" speeches![98]

A Changing Attitude

Next to King, Malcolm X was the decade's most influential black leader, and his views were in sharp contrast to those of King.

Martin Luther King delivers the "I Have a Dream" speech in August 1963. Although the speech inspired many, more militant black leaders felt disillusioned with nonviolent protest and advocated the use of force.

Malcolm X Rejects Nonviolence

If the Reverend Martin Luther King Jr. was the strongest advocate of nonviolence, Malcolm X was its greatest critic. In a speech in November 1963 in Detroit, he once again explained why he did not think blacks should practice nonviolence. It is taken from The Eyes on the Prize Civil Rights Reader, *edited by Clayborne Carson and others.*

As Reverend [Albert B.] Cleage [Jr.] pointed out, they say you should let your blood flow in the streets. This is a shame. You know he's a Christian preacher [but] there is nothing in our book, the Koran, that teaches us to suffer peacefully. Our [Muslim] religion teaches us to be intelligent. Be peaceful, be courteous, obey the law, respect everyone: but if someone puts his hand on you, send him to the cemetery. That's a good religion. In fact, that's that old-time religion. That's the one that Ma and Pa used to talk about: an eye for an eye, and a tooth for a tooth, and a head for a head, and a life for a life. That's a good religion. And nobody resents that kind of religion being taught but a wolf, who intends to make you his meal. This is the way it is with the white man in America. He's a wolf—and you're sheep. Any time a shepherd, a pastor, teaches you and me not to run from the white man and, at the same times, teaches us not to fight the white man, he's a traitor to you and me. Don't lay down a life all by itself. No. Preserve your life, it's the best thing you've got. And if you've got to give it up, let it be even-steven.

Malcolm X was the most famous militant black leader to reject nonviolence.

Malcolm disdained King's belief that nonviolence was the key to achieving black rights, claiming that "there is no philosophy more befitting the white man's tactics for keeping his foot on the black man's neck."[99] And Malcolm once said of King, "Any Negro who teaches other Negroes to turn the other cheek is disarming the Negro of his moral right, of his natural right, of his intelligent right to defend himself."[100]

Malcolm was not the only one to feel that way. Although nonviolence had been the foundation of the sit-ins, Freedom Rides, and other protests that slowly defeated southern segregation, many blacks in the 1960s turned away from that philosophy and embraced more radical, militant ideals and tactics to secure justice, including the use of force. Their mind-set changed because they were dismayed by continuing racist violence in the South, discouraged by the apathy of whites in other parts of America toward the economic and social problems of blacks, and angry that it was taking so long to gain their rights.

In the next few years after the March on Washington, cries of "Black Power!" replaced the gentle strains of the civil rights anthem "We Shall Overcome." Violence marred even protests that King led, and angry blacks rioted in northern cities. In a magazine article in 1966, Julius Lester, a former Student Nonviolent Coordinating Committee (SNCC) field secretary, summed up the new mood of young blacks whom he called "the angry children of Malcolm X": "This is their message: The days of singing freedom songs and the days of combating bullets and billy clubs with love are over. 'We Shall Overcome' sounds old, out-dated. Man, the people are too busy getting ready to fight to bother with singing any more!"[101]

Self-Defense

Nonviolence was a philosophy many blacks often found difficult to accept. Even the Reverend Fred Shuttlesworth, a cofounder with King of the Southern Christian Leadership Conference (SCLC), admitted that he practiced nonviolence mainly because he realized it was the only powerful tactic in the fight for civil rights. "I and others who might not have believed [in it]," he said, "accepted nonviolence as a principal tactic. We knew we couldn't fight the white man with guns and bombs and so forth."[102]

It was especially difficult to adhere to this philosophy when violence was directed at blacks. Some black leaders came to believe they should fight back. One of the earliest and most influential was Robert F. Williams, a former U.S. Marine who as head of the Monroe, North Carolina, chapter of the National Association for the Advancement of Colored People (NAACP) led protests to desegregate public facilities. But in 1959 the NAACP suspended Williams for six months for advocating violence against a white man who had raped a black woman but was declared innocent by a white jury. In the September

1959 issue of *Liberation* magazine, Williams claimed that physically attacking the rapist was the only way to punish him: "The great miscarriage of justice left me sick inside, and I said then what I say now. I believe Negroes must be willing to defend themselves, their women, their children, and their homes. They must be willing to die and to kill in repelling their assailants, Negroes *must* protect themselves."[103]

Williams put his radical philosophy into effect by creating an armed militia to defend blacks against whites. Williams so frightened North Carolina officials that in 1961 they concocted false charges that he had kidnapped a white couple, forcing him to flee the country. Although Williams spent the next eight years in exile in Cuba and China, returning home only after the charge was dropped, he continued to write articles and make radio broadcasts that advised blacks to arm themselves and fight back.

Malcolm X was equally blunt in advocating self-defense against whites. The Nation of Islam, whose members were called Black Muslims, believed that whites were their enemies. In a 1964 speech in New York City, Malcolm said violence was the only thing whites understood:

> You have to learn their language. Let's learn his language. If his language is with a shotgun, get a shotgun. Yes, I said if he only understands the language of a rifle, get a rifle. If he only understands the language of a rope, get a rope. But don't waste time talking the wrong language to a man if you want to really communicate with him. If something was wrong with that language [of violence], the federal government would have stopped [whites] from speaking it to you and me.[104]

SNCC Changes

Malcolm X's message rang true in 1963 when authorities allowed angry whites to use violence to safeguard segregation. Some of the decade's most brutal incidents occurred in May in Birmingham, Alabama, during protests King led. Under the direction of Public Safety Commissioner Eugene "Bull" Connor, police set loose attack dogs and used high-pressure hoses to knock down marchers, many of them children. In June, Medgar Evers, an NAACP leader in Jackson, Mississippi, was shot to death at his home. And on September 15, only eighteen days after the March on Washington, a bomb exploded at Birmingham's Sixteenth Street Baptist Church, killing four young girls attending a Bible class.

Such brutality made it increasingly difficult for many blacks to continue to accept nonviolence. Stokely Carmichael, who was elected SNCC chairman in 1966, once claimed that "King's error was that he tried to take nonviolence and make it a principle in a violent world."[105] Carmichael was a twenty-year-old Howard University student in 1961 when he became a Freedom Rider. Arrested in Jackson, Mississippi, Carmichael joined SNCC after serving a sentence at Parchman Prison.

Disciple of Violence

One of the first civil rights leaders to preach that blacks should arm themselves was Robert F. Williams, a former U.S. Marine. His views were controversial in the early 1960s, when most people still believed nonviolence could win blacks their rights. Williams, the former head of the Monroe, North Carolina, branch of the NAACP, was falsely charged with kidnapping. He fled the country to avoid arrest. In an article written in Cuba in June 1964, which was included in Black Protest Thought in the Twentieth Century, *edited by August Meier, Elliot Rudwick, and Francis Broderick, Williams defended his viewpoint and outlined weapons that blacks could use to fight whites.*

From the very earliest event of the African's chained arrival [as a slave] in the New World, he has been subjected to every form of brute force, systematic demoralization and dehumanization conceivable. The insensate slave masters left no stone unturned in condemning oppressed blacks to meekly accept their miserable lot. He was deliberately conditioned to base the prospects of his fortune on the Christian charity or conscience of the good white folks. Our people have never been allowed to forget that all significant power is in the hands of and under the control of the all-powerful God chosen by the white man. The weapons of defense employed by African-American freedom fighters must consist of a poor man's arsenal. Gasoline fire bombs (Molotov cocktails), lye or acid bombs can be used extensively. During the night hours, such weapons thrown from roof tops will make the streets impossible for racist cops to patrol. Hand grenades, bazookas, light mortars, rocket launchers, machine guns and ammunition can be bought clandestinely from servicemen anxious to make a fast dollar.

In the next few years, Carmichael and other SNCC members began to pull away from the concept of nonviolence upon which the group had been founded. They were influenced by Malcolm X and increasingly angered by racist attacks against them during peaceful protests. Julian Bond, who participated in the first sit-ins in Atlanta, Georgia, explains how most SNCC members began to change:

There came a point where we began to pull away from nonviolence, not just as a tactic but nonviolence period. Most of the people in my organization were wedded to nonviolence as a tactic. Strongly so. You are on the

Rescue workers remove a body from a church bombed in September 1963. As racist attacks increased, more and more blacks questioned the efficacy of nonviolent protest.

picket lines and somebody hits you, don't hit back. More and more we began to think that if I am walking down the street and somebody hits me, he better be ready because I am going to hit him back. Then more and more if I'm on the picket line and somebody hits me, I am not going to take it anymore. I think the nature of the work we did, the low pay we were getting, the negative experiences we had with government [not doing more to help blacks] just soured us on the chance of any progress being made using the techniques that King suggested.[106]

An example of SNCC's new mind-set came in Atlanta in September 1966 after police shot and wounded a black youth suspected of auto theft. When an angry crowd gathered, Carmichael went to the scene. Instead of trying to prevent violence by calming the angry blacks, Carmichael promised to return and help "tear this place apart."[107] Carmichael then sent SNCC workers back with a sound truck to lead the protest. When Mayor Ivan Allen Jr. asked the blacks to disperse, SNCC workers told them to ignore the mayor and to continue the protest, which erupted in violence. Afterward Police Chief Herbert Jenkins charged that SNCC should now be called "the Non-Student Violent Committee."[108]

Black Power

The official break with SNCC's peaceful past came on June 16, 1966, when Carmichael reached Greenwood, Mississippi, during a march to Jackson. James Meredith, who in 1962 had become the first black student at the University of Mississippi, had started the protest walk June 5 only to be wounded by a shotgun blast the next day. Afterward, several civil rights groups vowed to finish Meredith's walk.

Among, the marchers were King and Carmichael. When Carmichael arrived in Greenwood, he and several other people were arrested for ignoring police orders to erect tents at a black high school. After being released from jail, an angry Carmichael said: "This is the twenty-seventh time I have been arrested—and I ain't going to jail no more! The only way we gonna stop them white men from whuppin' is to take over. We been saying freedom for six years [since the sit-ins] and we ain't got nothin'. What we gonna start saying now is Black Power!"[109] The crowd began chanting the phrase over and over. During the rest of the march, those who embraced Carmichael's vision began to ridicule nonviolence by inserting new lines into the peace songs they had always sung. The lyrics now promised violence, such as "I'm gonna bomb when the spirit say bomb . . . cut when the spirit say cut . . . shoot when the spirit say shoot."[110]

"Black Power" soon became the rallying cry for blacks who had a new, more aggressive attitude about fighting racism. Instead of asking for their rights, they were now ready to demand them.

Stokely Carmichael delivers the speech that introduced the phrase "Black Power" to the world.

As Carmichael put it, "I'm not going to beg the white man for anything I deserve. I'm going to take it."[111]

Because Carmichael believed blacks must control their own destiny, he began to exclude whites from SNCC activities even though whites had always been a key part of the group. David Dawley, a white SNCC worker, remembers feeling betrayed by Carmichael's Black Power message: "Suddenly, I felt threatened. It seemed like a division between black and white. I was a 'honky [derisive term for white],' not 'David.'"[112] In the next few months, SNCC weeded out white SNCC workers in a move that alienated many people, including some blacks. SNCC's influence in the fight for civil rights began to diminish.

The same year Carmichael coined the phrase "Black Power," a new group arose that would come to symbolize the strident new militancy of many blacks. Its members were known as Black Panthers.

Black Panthers

The Black Panther Party was founded in Oakland, California, in October 1966 by Huey Newton and Bobby Seale, who met while attending Merritt Junior College. The group's original goal was to patrol black areas to protect residents from police brutality, a problem for blacks in all big cities. Newton explains why the Panthers did not accept nonviolence: "We had seen [King] come to Watts in an effort to calm the people [after a 1965 riot] and we had seen his philosophy of nonviolence rejected. Black people had been taught nonviolence, it was deep in us. What good, however, was nonviolence when the police were determined to rule by force?"[113]

Black Panthers like Newton, Seale, and Eldridge Cleaver were disciples of Malcolm X, but gradually they adopted views that were even more radical. The Panthers called for arming all blacks, the release of all blacks from jail, and financial compensation for blacks for slavery and the injustices they had endured in the century since slaves had been freed. The Panthers also made it clear they were willing to fight to achieve those goals. As Newton once claimed, "We're going to talk about political power growing out of the barrel of a gun."[114]

In California at that time, citizens could carry guns as long as they were not concealed, and the Black Panthers were always armed. Newspaper photographs of the warrior-like figures cradling rifles, shotguns, and pistols frightened whites but galvanized young blacks. Cleaver, who became the group's minister of information, remembered the first time he saw Black Panthers, in February 1967 in San Francisco, California:

I saw the most beautiful sight I had ever seen: four black men wearing black berets, powder blue shirts, black leather jackets, black trousers, shiny black shoes—and each with a gun! In front was Huey Newton with a riot pump shotgun in his

Black Panther Dances

Although the Black Panthers are best remembered today for violent clashes with law enforcement officials, the community programs they ran did a lot of good. In 1968 Regina Jennings, a black teenager who had left home at the age of fifteen, moved from Philadelphia, Pennsylvania, to Oakland, California, to join the Panthers. Jennings was involved in many of the social events the Panthers sponsored to help local blacks, such as free breakfasts for schoolchildren. In The Black Panther Party (Reconsidered), *edited by Charles E. Jones, she discusses a little-known example of Panther community work.*

People may not know about the dances we staged for the Oakland youth. We decorated the community centers, halls, or church basements with our colors—blue and black. We hung blue and black streamers and lights and Panther paraphernalia on walls. On tables, there were the usual posters and buttons of our national leaders, Kathleen Cleaver, Eldridge Cleaver, Bobby Seale, and Huey P. Newton. We sisters attempted to bake cakes and cookies but we were not very good cooks, and the common people knew it. They usually supplied the food for our dances. When not on guard duty, we jammed on the dance floor with one another or with community brothers and sisters. Sometimes young males would rap to us sisters while we were dancing under blue [and] black lights, and we would laugh and urge them to join the party. Local Panther male leaders made speeches after playing records— the Isley Brothers, Sly Stone, James Brown—and the youth pretty much listened attentively. Whether or not they joined our organization, we usually won community sympathizers after our events.

Black Panthers march in New York City. The Panthers instituted many community programs that benefited black neighborhoods.

right hand, barrel pointed down to the floor; beside him was Bobby Seale, the handle of a .45-caliber automatic showing from its holster on his right hip.[115]

Although on the surface the Panthers seemed dedicated only to violence, the chapters in Oakland and other cities, like Chicago, Illinois, began providing free services to blacks, including health care, meals, and classes in basic education. Such programs were commendable, but when David Hilliard of the Panthers discussed them he always used militant terms, claiming that the humanitarian activities were part of a "survival program" and "an activity that strengthens us for the coming fight."[116]

Despite the group's good work, the aggressive jargon members used and the fact that they were always armed made them a target for police and the Federal Bureau of Investigation, which began considering the Panthers a threat to national security. The result was a series of armed conflicts in Oakland, New York, Chicago, and other cities that killed many Panthers and sent others to prison; one was Newton, who was charged with killing a policeman in one shootout. By the end of the 1960s the Panthers were on the decline, their chapters were weakened, and they were no longer effective in helping blacks.

Riots

In the summer of 1966, angry blacks rioted in northern cities like Chicago, Detroit, Michigan, and Newark, New Jersey.

However, that summer was not the first in which violence had swept through ghettos, the run-down, segregated areas in big cities where most blacks lived.

The decade's first major riot came in 1964 in Harlem, a section of New York City where many blacks lived. Like many of the outbreaks that followed in the next few years, it was sparked by trouble with police, who shot and killed a fifteen-year-old black youth while trying to arrest him. What began on July 18 as a peaceful Congress of Racial Equality (CORE) rally against that alleged police brutality turned into a riot as blacks, carried away by their anger over the incident and police conduct in general, destroyed property and looted stores. Before it ended five days later, 1 black had been killed, 500 arrested, 140 injured along with dozens of whites, and tens of millions of dollars' worth of damage had been done.

The Reverend Bernard Lee of the SCLC traveled with King to Harlem after the riots. According to Lee, Harlem blacks rejected King's peaceful philosophy: "The word nonviolence turned them off. Harlem was a different world for us. They [big-city blacks] always saw nonviolence as the sissy way out, the weak way out, the do-nothing way out."[117] Northern blacks seemed to have more bottled-up anger than southern blacks, mainly over the conditions that surrounded them—the run-down tenements, poor schools, and lack of decent jobs. This anger sparked riots every summer for the next four years, giving rise to the term "long hot summer" to describe the season of violence.

What is considered the twentieth century's worst race riot happened in Detroit in 1967. Ron Scott, an auto worker, said blacks simply exploded in anger on July 23 after police forcibly tried to break up a party. "Inside of most blacks was a time bomb," said Scott. "There was rage that [began] to come out."[118]

Albert Wilson was thirteen years old when the altercation between blacks and police erupted into five days of rioting and looting. He vividly remembers how joyous people were while they took part in the terrible events: "It was kind of like a carnival, a parade, a party, because everybody there was laughing. I saw people

The Deacons of Defense

In 1964 in Bogalusa, Louisiana, Charles R. Sims founded the Deacons for Defense and Justice, the first organized black self-protection group. In My Soul Is Rested: Movement Days in the Deep South Remembered *by Howell Raines, Sims explains the decision to organize and arm blacks to protect them against racist white.*

One afternoon two civil rights workers were attacked by six whites in a black neighborhood. We captured the whites and kept 'em 'til the police arrived, and the police turned them loose. Then we decided since we didn't have the protection from the law, by the law, we should organize a group to protect our peoples in the neighborhood. So we organized a group [and] we started callin' 'em the Deacons. And we took up the job of self-defense. I'd like to explain one thing about the Deacons. We never attacked anyone, but we would defend ourselves against anybody at any time, anywhere, regardless of the price.

In addition to defending black neighborhoods against whites, Sims explained to Raines how his group protected blacks who protested against segregation.

The whole city was resistin' the Civil Rights Act, such as public accommodations, the right to set up a picket line picketing merchants for jobs. It's eighteen pickets walkin' the picket line, and you look up, and in fifteen or twenty minutes, you got three, four hundred whites harassin' 'em. That calls the Deacons out automatically, and we'd go out. [And] they know we had nerve enough to walk among them and we didn't give no ground, and if we'da had to, we'd fight right there, in that huddle.

running from stores with televisions but with a smile on their face. Everybody was happy."[119] The riot ended only after heavily armed National Guard soldiers entered the city to quiet things down. The toll was immense—forty-one people died, an estimated six hundred were injured, and property losses hit $45 million, with most of the damage to buildings set on fire. One of the injured was Wilson, who was struck in the spine by a police bullet while he was inside a store with other blacks. He was paralyzed for life, never able to walk again.

Trouble in Memphis

The pent-up resentment over past and present injustices gave rise to the riots and began to mar civil rights protests. Such disorder even tarnished the reputation of King, the champion of nonviolence.

On March 28, 1968, King was in Memphis, Tennessee, to lead a protest march on behalf of striking sanitation workers. Several militant groups were also involved including the Invaders, a violent group armed with weapons. Before the march, one Invader claimed, "If you expect honkies [whites] to get

Fires burn during the 1967 Detroit riots. Forty-one people died and six hundred were injured during the altercation between police and black protesters.

the message, you got to break some windows."[120]

On the day of the march, when King saw the mood of the crowd of some seven thousand people, he realized trouble would erupt. "I can't lead a violent march. Call it off,"[121] King told the SCLC's Jim Lawson. Lawson tried, but failed. What was intended as a peaceful march became a riot as blacks damaged buildings, looted stores, and fought with police, including exchanges of gunfire; in the end, 280 people were arrested, 60 injured, and a sixteen-year-old black youth was shot to death by police.

King knew he would be blamed for the riot even though other blacks had led the protesters into violence. "This is terrible," he said. "Now we'll never get anyone to believe in nonviolence."[122] As he feared, southern newspapers eagerly proclaimed that the incident proved that King no longer advocated nonviolence.

A Poor Farewell

Ironically, some of the worst riots of the decade would break out because of King. The great civil rights leader was shot to death in Memphis on April 4, 1968, while standing on the balcony of his room at the Lorraine Motel. The assassin was James Earl Ray, a career criminal.

The reaction to King's death was anger and hatred. In Washington, D.C., Carmichael told blacks to "get your guns" because "when white America killed Dr. King, she declared war on us."[123] Many other blacks felt the same way; riots broke out in 110 cities across the nation, causing massive destruction and thirty-nine deaths. The response to King's death went against everything he stood for. In 1964, when King accepted the Nobel Peace Prize in Oslo, Norway, he had commented on mankind's need to change: "Nonviolence is the answer to the crucial political and moral questions of our time. Man must evolve for all human conflict a method which rejects revenge, aggression, and retaliation. The foundation of such a method is love."[124] But as both blacks and whites continually discovered as the decade went on, it was much harder to respond to enemies with love than with hate and violence. That was something even King understood.

White Backlash: Resisting the Civil Rights Movement

On the night of May 11, 1963, a bomb heavily damaged the Birmingham, Alabama, home of the Reverend A.D. (Alfred Daniel) King, the younger brother of the Reverend Martin Luther King Jr. Shortly after that, another explosive device rocked the city's A.C. Gaston Motel, headquarters of the Southern Christian Leadership Conference (SCLC) while it led antisegregation protests. Four people were injured by the hotel blast, but A.D. King and his family escaped harm. Although King asked God to forgive whoever detonated the bomb, he knew the reason behind the cowardly attack. "Violence," he said, "has always been the tactic of the white man." [125]

The bombings were the angry reaction by racists to a May 10 agreement in which local merchants had agreed to desegregate lunch counters and hire black workers in clerical and sales positions. Unwilling to accept the victory blacks had won, whites resorted to violence to intimidate and punish blacks fighting for their rights.

The bombs, beatings, shootings, and slayings that violently punctuated civil rights history in the 1960s created shocking headlines, brutal television footage, and widespread moral outrage across America. These barbarous acts did not stop blacks from gaining their rights. However, the obstinate refusal of state and local governments to accept integration, even when the federal government ordered it, were much more effective. Southern elected officials, all of whom were white in that period, ignored federal orders to stop segregating public places, harassed and jailed blacks who were peacefully protesting, and allowed white violence against blacks.

John Patterson, Alabama's attorney general from 1954 to 1960 and its governor for the next two years, admits that he and other officials were simply trying to delay what they knew was inevitable—a black civil rights victory. Patterson said that to avoid school integration, Alabama and other southern states created laws that made it difficult for blacks to win court orders to force black and white students to attend school together:

An effort was made to get legislation passed to decentralize control of the school systems to make [blacks] file a multitude of suits rather than taking us on in one suit and integrating all the schools at one time. Our whole program of delay was to [stall any action] because we knew we were going to lose. This was our whole idea, and it worked for me for eight years.[126]

Alabama governor John Patterson admitted that many southern states created laws aimed at preventing blacks from securing civil rights.

While officials tried to use legal and political means to delay civil rights gains, racist whites resorted to violence to accomplish the same goal. The most barbaric and hateful were members of the Ku Klux Klan (KKK), the white supremacist group that had been waging a terrorist war against blacks since shortly after the end of the Civil War.

KKK

The Ku Klux Klan was started in 1866 by former Confederate soldiers in Pulaski, Tennessee; other units soon spread across the South. The first two words of its name—*Ku Klux*—were a corruption of the Greek word for "circle"—*kyklos*—and the last was "clan" spelled with a *K*. The Klan became an underground resistance force that used violence to oppose U.S. government officials and soldiers who occupied the defeated South during Reconstruction, which lasted until 1876.

During Reconstruction, blacks had the rights of other citizens, including being able to vote, but after Reconstruction, state and local governments passed laws taking those rights away. Klan members, believing blacks were inferior to whites, also tried to restore their ideal of white supremacy through intimidation and violence against newly freed blacks. In nighttime raids in which they dressed in sheets to avoid being identified, they beat blacks to make them subservient and sometimes killed them.

A century later in the 1960s, the KKK, fueled by anger that blacks were finally gaining their rights, was stronger than ever. And Klan members still believed that it was proper to use violence to keep blacks in their place. Warren Folks, who headed a Klan unit in Jacksonville, Florida, told *Life* magazine in 1965:

I believe in the Klan. I don't believe the thing to do at this moment is to go out and shoot a nigger in the street, but when the time comes—when it comes—we'll take them down by the busload, by the trainload, that's what we'll do. By the busload. By the carload! We don't hate Negroes. We love 'em, in their place—like shinin' shoes, bell-hoppin', pickin' cotton, diggin' ditches, eatin' possum, servin' time [in prison], etc.[127]

KKK Violence

In the 1960s the various groups that operated under the overall banner of the KKK were collectively called the "Invisible Empire." This nickname arose because it was hard to know who the group's members were because they often wore white robes in public to shield their identity.

Many people, black and white, did fear those nameless, faceless vigilantes because the KKK was responsible for most of the decade's civil rights violence. Charles McDew admits that he and other Student Nonviolent Coordinating Committee (SNCC) workers were intimidated by a Klan greeting when they entered Mississippi in 1961: "I remember we stopped at the border and there was a big sign that said, 'The Knights of the Ku Klux Klan welcome you to Mississippi,' and we grew silent and we all were very afraid. And we knew that we were about to walk into the heart of the beast."[128]

KKK members engaged in many different types of activities in their often violent attempts to preserve segregation between blacks and whites. They heckled sit-in protesters, beat Freedom Riders, shot to death civil rights workers both white and black, and made bombs that destroyed property and took innocent lives. The Klan, in fact, held classes in bomb making.

The Klan often staged public rallies to intimidate blacks, giving racist speeches and burning crosses, a traditional warning that the Klan was ready to strike. The bomb that damaged A.D. King's home exploded only a few hours after a KKK rally outside the city. One of the speakers at the rally was Robert Shelton, Imperial Wizard of the United Klans of America. Claiming the concessions blacks had won in Birmingham "are not worth the paper they're written on," Shelton went on to threaten that "Martin Luther King's epitaph [an inscription on a tombstone], in my opinion, can be written here in Birmingham."[129] As in many violent incidents in the South, no one was arrested.

The Klan used its violent deeds to intimidate southern whites sympathetic to blacks, including elected officials. Connie Curry, the first white member of SNCC's executive committee, remembers how frightened she was during a sit-in in Atlanta when she realized that she was standing next to the Grand Dragon, one of the top leaders of the Georgia Klan. Said Curry:

> When the sit-inners were turned down [for service] Calvin Craig had just handed me a little leaflet, and he was [cursing the blacks.] I was standing there saying, "Dear God, please don't let [other SNCC activists] show any recognition when they come out of the Magnolia Room 'cause Calvin Craig will surely kill me.[130]

In Bogalusa, Louisiana, a city nicknamed "Klantown, USA" because of its racism, the Klan in 1965 assaulted blacks and burned their homes in an attempt to stop their campaign to desegregate public facilities. When a federal court held a hearing on an injunction against Klan activity, Mayor Jesse H. Cutrer Jr. testified how frightened he had been when he went to a Klan meeting in an attempt to get Klansmen to end the violence. "All I could see was their eyes. I was frightened. You can't be too comfortable talking to a group of eyes," Cutrer said about seeing 150 Klansmen dressed in white robes.[131]

Racist Lawmen

That fear of unknown Klansmen and what they might do often kept public officials from supporting civil rights. However, many elected officials held the same racist views as the KKK and some were even

Racist Hatred

It is hard today for most people to imagine how deeply some whites hated blacks in the 1960s. Such mindless racism was revealed in a speech by the Reverend Conley Lynch of St. Petersburg, Florida, at a Ku Klux Klan rally in St. Augustine, Florida, on September 18, 1963. His comments to four hundred Klansmen concerned the deaths three days earlier of four girls—Cynthia Wesley, Denise McNair, Carol Robertson, and Addie Mae Collins—killed in the bombing of the Sixteenth Street Baptist Church in Birmingham, Alabama. His speech is taken from The Fiery Cross: The Ku Klux Klan in America *by Wyn Craig Wade.*

I'll tell you people here tonight, if they can find those fellows [who bombed the church] they ought to pin medals on them. Someone said, "Ain't it a shame that them little children was killed?" In the first place, they ain't little. They're fourteen or fifteen years old [one was eleven and three fourteen]. In the second place they weren't children. Children are little people, little human beings and that means white people. There's little dogs and cats and apes and baboons and skunks and there's also little niggers. But they ain't children. They're just little niggers. And in the third place, it wasn't no shame they was killed. Why? Because when I go out to kill rattlesnakes, I don't make no difference between little rattlesnakes and big rattlesnakes, because I know it is the nature of all rattlesnakes to be my enemies and to poison me if they can. So I kill 'em all. . . . I say, "Good for whoever planted the bomb!" We're all better off. I believe in violence, all the violence it takes either to scare [them] out of the country or to have 'em all six feet under!

Ku Klux Klan members march in Georgia. Throughout the 1960s, Klansmen held a profound and violent hatred for blacks.

members of the Klan. This included law enforcement officials on the city, county, and state levels, many of whom had been elected to protect citizens—by white voters.

One of the most infamous was Eugene "Bull" Connor, who as Commissioner of Public Safety ran the Birmingham fire and police departments. In 1961, when a bus loaded with Freedom Riders arrived in Birmingham, he sent no police to protect them even though federal officials had warned him of possible violence. A hostile crowd beat up many of the riders. Connor claimed he did not have enough officers to send because it was Mother's Day, and they were all visiting their moms. He also blamed the riders for the violence: "The people of Birmingham are a peaceful people, and we never have any trouble here unless some people come into our city looking for trouble."[132]

Yet in the spring of 1963, Connor was able to mobilize a huge force of police officers and firefighters to deal with blacks marching for their rights. In one of the decade's most brutal displays of police power, Connor loosed attack dogs on marchers, many of them children, and ordered firefighters to wield high-pressure hoses against protesters. When the Reverend Fred Shuttlesworth was knocked unconscious by a powerful stream of water, Connor commented, "I waited a week to see Shuttlesworth get hit with a hose: I'm sorry I missed it. I wish

Eugene "Bull" Connor was one of many elected officials in the South who tried to foil the efforts of civil rights activists.

they'd carried him away in a hearse."[133]

Connor's racism was shared by many law officers. Prathia Hall, a SNCC field-worker, who helped blacks register to vote, remembers how one official nearly shot her in Sasser, Georgia:

One day four of us were confronted by a guy with a tin badge on [who] said he was the marshal. He came up to us and he wanted to know, "What are you doing?" and I said, "We're registering people to vote and you have no right to stop us." And he went *mad*. I mean, really mad, and he began cursing and calling us all these names and literally foaming at the mouth. He pulled out a pistol and began firing bullets in a circle around my feet. And the only thing that I can be thankful for is that I didn't move.[134]

Not all police, however, supported the Klan. Obie Clark, a teacher in Meridian, Mississippi, active in civil rights, said Police Chief Roy Gunn warned blacks several times about planned KKK attacks on homes and churches, enabling blacks to defend the property. "Police Chief Gunn, he had some people [informants] inside the Klan, and we were ready for them in most instances," said Clark. "We foiled a lot of their plans in Meridian because of that."[135] Some whites punished Gunn by targeting his home for a bombing.

George Wallace

The reason local officials like Connor could act as they did was that the governors of their states shared their racism. Connor's beliefs were supported by Alabama governor George Wallace, who in his 1963 inaugural address pledged he would never quit fighting civil rights:

It is very appropriate then that from this Cradle of the Confederacy, this very heart of the great Anglo-Saxon Southland, that today we sound the drum for freedom. . . . In the name of the greatest people that have ever trod this earth, I draw the line in the dust and toss the gauntlet before the feet of tyranny [the federal government]. And I say, Segregation now! Segregation tomorrow! Segregation forever![136]

John Patterson, who had defeated Wallace in the 1958 gubernatorial campaign, had also tried to stop black rights. One of his most obvious attempts was to deny protection to the Freedom Riders, relenting only when President John F. Kennedy and Attorney General Robert F. Kennedy personally pressured him into doing so. Patterson had defeated Wallace by winning the endorsement of the KKK, but afterwards Wallace made a vow to a campaign aide: "I was out-niggered, and I will never be out-niggered again."[137] By that, Wallace meant he would never again allow another opponent to take a tougher stand against blacks than he did.

When Wallace was elected in 1962, he kept his promise to resist civil rights for blacks. Wallace allowed local officials in Birmingham and Selma to prosecute blacks who peacefully protested and to beat them while they were being arrested. He ignored KKK activities, claimed blacks were causing the violence, and refused to honor federal court orders on integration. His resistance to the federal courts involved him in one of the decade's most dramatic confrontations.

Malone and Hood

Like other southern states, Alabama fought to keep blacks out of its state universities. When a federal court issued an order to enroll Vivian Malone and James A. Hood in the University of Alabama's summer session, Wallace vowed to "stand in the schoolhouse door"[138] and stop such integration by barring enrollment of any black students.

On June 11, 1963, Wallace fulfilled his pledge, standing with his arm upraised in the doorway of the campus building in which students registered. Accompanied by federal marshals, Malone and Hood simply detoured around him to their dormitories. Several hours later, when three thousand soldiers of the Alabama National Guard arrived on the campus in Tuscaloosa on orders from President Kennedy, Wallace quietly left and the students were registered. Wallace's brief but dramtic defiance made him famous across the country and a hero to people who opposed integration. He would capitalize on his celebrity in several campaigns for president, including one in 1968 in which he drew over 9.9 million votes and won five states. Wallace's defiant stand, however, had been staged mostly for the news media. Wallace knew that Kennedy

Alabama governor George Wallace (at podium) blocks the doorway of a University of Alabama campus building to prevent two black students from enrolling at the school.

would dispatch troops to the campus and that the students' enrollment was inevitable.

Although Malone and Hood registered peacefully, racist students made their stay difficult. Malone, who attended Alabama until her graduation in 1965, said student life was often unpleasant: "I would walk across the campus to the Commerce Department [building], and some of the students would say, 'Here comes our nigger,' and they'd laugh. But I was never physically hurt."[139] One reason Malone was not injured was that she was guarded by federal marshals the entire time she was a student. And even though Malone had to endure insults, her experience was not as bad as that of James Meredith, the first black admitted to a white southern university.

James Meredith

On September 3, 1962, a federal judge ordered the University of Mississippi to admit Meredith, an air force veteran then attending Jackson State, a black school. In his book *Three Years in Mississippi*, Meredith admitted that in transferring, "my purpose was to break the system of 'white supremacy.'"[140] Governor Ross Barnett immediately understood the threat Meredith posed to segregation and in a televised speech promised to fight his admission: "There is no case in history where the Caucasian race has survived social integration. We must either submit to the unlawful dictate of the federal government or stand up like men and tell them, 'Never.'"[141]

Like Wallace a year later, Barnett tried to stall Meredith's entry as long as possible even though he knew the federal government was strong enough to enforce the court order. On September 20, when Meredith tried to register, Barnett personally blocked his way and he did it again five days later. Throughout the month, federal officials had been in contact with Barnett to try to find a peaceful end to the stalemate. When Barnett refused to bend, the president called Mississippi's National Guard into federal service on September 29 and ordered troops to be ready, if necessary, to accompany Meredith as he enrolled.

Protected by three hundred federal officials, Meredith arrived at the Oxford campus on September 30 and was taken to his dormitory. While he slept safely, a riot ensued as several hundred racist whites first taunted and then began to fight with the marshals, who used tear gas to disperse the mob. The fighting grew worse and gunshots were exchanged before the president finally called in soldiers to end the riot. Two civilians were shot to death—French reporter Paul Guihard and Ray Gunter, an Oxford resident who was watching events unfold—and 166 marshals were injured, 28 of them by gunshots.

The violence never reached Meredith. In fact, he had no idea how bad it was until the next day:

When the trouble started, I could not see or hear very much of it. Most of the events occurred at the other end of the campus, and I did not look out

White Officials Against Blacks

In 1963 and 1964, Michael Thelwell was a SNCC field secretary in Mississippi. In A Circle of Trust: Remembering SNCC *by Cheryl Lynn Greenberg, Thelwell comments on how frightening it was for blacks to live in a place where elected officials, from police officers to judges trying cases, were against them.*

The cops didn't have to respect [blacks]. I remember in Canton, when the sheriff would go in and deputize all the drunkards in the bars on Saturday night—the garbage men, rednecks, drunks—it's 12 o'clock and they're deputizing them, giving them badges, sticks, and guns and sending them out to cope with black people. Where the murder of somebody black wasn't a crime. Trying to impanel a jury to try the murderer of [civil rights leader] Medgar Evers who was being [honored and celebrated] up and down Highway 49 in every bar he went. People would buy him drinks as he told them how he had assassinated Medgar Evers. Trying to impanel the jury, the federal prosecutor asked the prospective jurors, all of whom were white since they are taken from the voters list, "Do you think it's a crime for a white man to kill a Negro?" . . . One old white farmer was the most honest in terms of his answers. He said, "Well, that depends on what [he] done done." What I want you to envision is the sense of absolute and total vulnerability that American citizens had who happened to be black, knowing that none of the institutions of society existed on their behalf or would protect them.

As Thelwell noted, officials did not care about even the murder of a black person. Byron de la Beckwith was tried twice for shooting Evers, but both times juries failed to reach a verdict, which meant that the charges were dropped.

the window. I think I read a newspaper and went to bed around ten o'clock. I was awakened several times in the night by the noise and shooting outside, but I had no way of knowing what was going on [and] I slept pretty well all night.[142]

Meredith attended the University of Mississippi until his 1963 graduation. Because of death threats, Meredith had to be guarded by federal marshals and soldiers the entire time. One racist letter Meredith received contained a piece of singed rope, a reminder that whites in the past had lynched and burned blacks, and a short poem: "Roses are red, violets are blue; I've killed one nigger and might as well make it two."[143]

Lester Maddox

After being elected governor, both Wallace and Barnett became famous for opposing civil rights. But in 1966 Lester Maddox was elected governor *because of* the celebrity he had earned by refusing to serve blacks at his Atlanta restaurant on July 3, 1964, one day after President Lyndon B. Johnson signed the Civil Rights Act outlawing discrimination in public places.

Maddox had never allowed black diners in several restaurants he owned, including the Pickrick, which served hamburgers and fried chicken. During the 1960s,

Maddox even used Pickrick ads to criticize people who favored integration because he believed the mixing of the races was wrong. In one ad, Maddox responded to a letter from someone who favored civil rights: "I do hope you'll get your integration wishes—a stomach full of race mixing, and lap full of little mulatto [mixed black and white] grandchildren, so you can run your fingers through their hair."[144]

When five black ministers tried to enter the Pickrick on July 3 in an effort to integrate the restaurant, Maddox went wild; he threatened them with a revolver and hit the top of their car with an ax handle as it pulled away. The incident created national headlines and earned Maddox admiration from segregationists. Maddox

A white majority elected Lester Maddox (right) as governor of Georgia after he refused to serve blacks at his whites-only restaurant in Atlanta.

even began selling ax handles to his admirers for two dollars apiece. After a legal battle ended on February 5, 1965, with a court order forcing Maddox to serve blacks, he closed the restaurant rather than integrate it.

His stand made him so popular that in 1966, with the backing of the KKK, he was elected governor. But in his inaugural speech, Maddox surprised Georgians with conciliatory words on civil rights. "There will be no place in Georgia during the next four years," he said, "for those who advocate extremism or violence."[145] And to the wonder of many, as governor from 1967 to 1971 Maddox did not act like a racist. Maddox appointed the first black to head a state department (the Board of Corrections), named the first blacks as state troopers and state investigators, and even ordered troopers to quit calling blacks by racist terms.

Maddox was so evenhanded in treating blacks that he won the praise of civil rights leader Hosea Williams, a former aide to the Reverend Martin Luther King Jr. Years later, when Williams was a Georgia state legislator, he introduced a bill to give a penniless Maddox a state pension, saying, "He talked that racist talk, but the walk he walked was much different."[146] Maddox's transformation mystified most people. A common theory about his change in attitude was that Maddox had pretended to be racist in the past to lure white customers to his restaurant and to get them to vote him into office.

One Repents, One Does Not

Although victory in the battle for civil rights was as inevitable as it was morally right, many racists never accepted it. In an interview with author Patsy Sims in her 1996 book *The Klan*, Klan leader Shelton's only regret was that whites did not fight hard enough to stop blacks: "It's unfortunate, really, that there wasn't more violence than what it was. I feel like had there been enough violence, it would have stopped all of this, and we wouldn't be in the position we're in today [with the races integrated]."[147] But George Wallace was one of the southerners who was able to admit he had been wrong. In 1982 at a meeting in Birmingham of the SCLC, Wallace made amends for his past opposition to civil rights: "I did stand, with a majority of the white people, for the separation of the schools. But that was wrong, and that will never come back again."[148]

Black Pride:
A New Mood Sweeps
the Nation

In 1903 W.E.B. Du Bois wrote *The Souls of Black Folk*, a collection of thirteen essays and short stories that even a century later are considered among the most powerful and eloquent ever penned about the racial divide between blacks and whites. Du Bois explains how difficult it was to be black in the United States:

> One ever feels his two-ness—an American, a Negro; two souls, two thoughts, two unreconciled strivings; two warring ideals in one dark body, whose dogged strength alone keeps it from being torn asunder. He simply wishes to make it possible for a man to be both a Negro and an American, without being cursed and spit upon by his fellow, without having the door of opportunity closed roughly in his face.[149]

Du Bois was commenting on the harsh truth that blacks were not equal to whites in a country that boasted of having been founded on the most powerful promise in the Declaration of Independence, that "all men are created equal." This sense of inequality was beaten into blacks daily by racist whites. For black children, the first incident that made them realize whites considered them inferior was etched in their memories forever. Charles Jones, who was born in 1937 in Chester, South Carolina, remembers learning this terrible truth as a child by witnessing how a white pharmacist treated a black teacher:

> The pharmacist counted out the pills and handed the prescription to the woman. "Thank you," she said. "Thank you what?" said the pharmacist. "Thank you," she said, again. "Thank you, *sir*," corrected the pharmacist. The teacher said, "I beg your pardon," and he slapped her right hard, and told her that any time she came in there to refer to him as "sir" because he was white.[150]

It was a bitter lesson for a youngster. Thurgood Marshall, who on October 2, 1967, was sworn in as the U.S. Supreme Court's first black justice, commented once on how such incidents affected young blacks: "The Negro child is branded in his own mind as inferior; he thus acquires a roadblock in his mind which prevents his ever feeling that he is equal."[151]

It was in such ways that racism had been warping and destroying the self-image blacks had of themselves ever since 1619, when a Dutch ship brought the first blacks to America as slaves. The civil rights movement was not only about freeing blacks physically to sit next to whites in restaurants or cast votes in elections alongside whites. The battle was also about liberating them from the psychological and emotional shackles of racism so they could become unafraid of whites and aware that they were as good as anyone else.

Black Pride

The twisted, negative attitudes some whites had about blacks—that they were lazy, stupid, and immoral—were reinforced culturally by the way blacks were portrayed in movies, history books, and the news media. James Farmer, a founder of the Congress of Racial Equality (CORE), believed that such biased characterizations had helped cause "the black man to reject himself and even hate himself."[152]

Some blacks were so poisoned by white society's negative attitude toward them that they became ashamed of being black, leading them to use chemicals to lighten their skin or straighten their naturally kinky hair in order to conform to white ideals of beauty. As a young man, Malcolm X, who did as much as anyone in the 1960s to help blacks rediscover their racial pride, straightened his own hair in a style known as a "conk." With the help of a friend, Shorty, he applied a mixture that contained lye, eggs, potatoes, and Vaseline. Malcolm explains the process as not only painful but, as he later realized, degrading: "I gritted my teeth and tried to pull the sides of the kitchen table together. My eyes watered, my nose ran. I couldn't stand it any longer; I bolted to the washbasin. I was cursing Shorty with every name I could think of when he got the spray going and started soap-lathering my head." Years later, Malcolm understood that many blacks had been "so brainwashed into believing that black people are 'inferior'—and white people

Identifying with Tarzan

Before the 1960s, the confusion many young blacks felt about their racial identity even carried over to their movie screen heroes. James Farmer, a founder of CORE and originator of the 1961 Freedom Rides, admitted in a 1968 speech at Syracuse University that when he watched Tarzan movies, he rooted for the white jungle hero when he battled African natives. This excerpt from Farmer's speech is from Black Protest Thought in the Twentieth Century, *edited by August Meier, Elliott Rudwick, and Francis Broderick.*

We had rejected Africa, and that had been part of the self-rejection too. For we had, as most Americans had, the Hollywood image of Africa. And we are all familiar with that image—a few half-naked black savages dancing around a boiling pot with a missionary in it. That was the way we saw Africa, and a common saying in the black community was, "Man, I ain't no African." We would go to the movies to watch the Tarzan pictures and with whom did we identify? With Tarzan, of course. We'd say, "Kill that savage, Tarzan, kill him." . . . Kill me, Tarzan. As a child in Austin [Texas], about ten years of age, my buddy and I would go down to the movie every Saturday to watch the half hour Tarzan serial. We had to see our hero; we couldn't miss a single week. We would watch the missionary in the pot with the sweat dripping from his brow as the heat built up underneath and he awaited the inevitable and timely arrival of Tarzan. They would show the Africans dancing around the pot to the tom-tom beat; then they would flash on the screen a close-up of the face of one of the Africans, all painted and fierce. Then I'd elbow my buddy and say, "Irving, that's you." [And Irving would say] "No, man, that ain't me. I didn't come from Africa."

Many young blacks of the 1960s identified more with Tarzan than with the African natives he fought.

'superior'—that they will even violate and mutilate their God-created bodies to try to look 'pretty' by white standards."[153]

The feelings of inferiority and self-hatred some blacks felt changed dramatically in the sixties as civil rights victories helped blacks gain a new sense of pride. As head of the Student Nonviolent Coordinating Committee (SNCC), Stokely Carmichael had coined the phrase "Black Power." But he firmly believed that before blacks could gain political and economic power, they had to become proud of themselves: "It is time to stop being ashamed of being black. It is time to stop trying to be white. When you see your daughter playing in the fields, with her nappy hair, and her wide nose, and her thick lips, tell her she is beautiful. *Tell your daughter she is beautiful.*"[154] Comments such as that by Carmichael and other black leaders popularized the phrase "Black Is Beautiful," and blacks began to appreciate their unique physical characteristics. Many blacks allowed their hair to grow long, reveling in the bushy, stylish "Afros" that symbolized their newfound pride in being black.

Malcolm X

But before blacks could begin to respect themselves, they had to resolve the mixed, sometimes bitter feelings they had toward whites, who for centuries had enslaved them, denied them their rights, and treated them as second-class citizens. Many blacks, in a misguided attempt to quit feeling inferior to whites, began to resent them. No black leader expressed that emotion more powerfully than Malcolm X.

Born Malcolm Little on May 19, 1925, in Omaha, Nebraska, he knew violence at a young age. When Malcolm was six years old, his father, Earl, a Baptist minister, was beaten to death by whites. Although a good student, Malcolm quit school after seventh grade and fell into a life of crime. While serving a burglary sentence at the Norfolk Prison Colony in Massachusetts, Malcolm began to read a lot and take correspondence courses to learn more. Malcolm also realized that heavy drinking, the crimes he had committed, and other immoral aspects of his life had been wrong, and he began searching for a way to become a better person.

Malcolm found the key to his salvation when his brother, Philbert, visited him in prison in 1948 and introduced him to the teachings of the Nation of Islam, which Elijah Muhammad had started in Detroit, Michigan, in 1930. Members had to convert to the Muslim religion, thus giving them their nickname of "Black Muslims." When Malcolm was released from prison in 1952, he joined the Nation of Islam. Malcolm explains why he then changed his last name:

I wasn't born Malcolm Little. Little is the name of the slave master who owned one of my grandparents during slavery, a white man, and the name Little was handed down to my grandfather, to my father and on to me. But [after] realizing that Little is

Malcolm X inspired blacks to take pride in the color of their skin and he encouraged all blacks to join together in the fight for civil rights.

an English name, and I'm not an Englishman, I gave the Englishman back his name; and since my own had been stripped from me, hidden from me, and I don't know it, I use X.[155]

Malcolm's Influence

By joining the Black Muslims and changing his name, Malcolm X had taken important steps in developing pride in being black. There were fewer than four hundred Black Muslims then, but in the next two decades Malcolm helped the group attract thousands of converts by appealing to their desire to believe they were as good as anyone else, no matter what the color of their skin. A powerful and eloquent speaker, Malcolm and his ideas became popular with many blacks. "There is some [Black] Muslim in a whole lot of Negroes,"[156] he boasted.

One of his most powerful messages was his repeated call for black unity: "My black brothers and sisters—of all religious beliefs or of no religious beliefs—we all have in common the greatest binding tie we could have . . . we are all black people!"[157] This concept of black nationalism meant that blacks should consider themselves a unified force and band together to better conditions for themselves.

Malcolm's ideas about taking pride in being black heavily influenced many other blacks, including civil rights leaders Carmichael and Eldridge Cleaver, the Black Panther Party leader who, like Malcolm X, also had a profound change of character while in prison. Sonia Sanchez, a New York City poet who was active in CORE, explains that Malcolm's message resonated with many blacks because he made them feel good about themselves: "That's why we all loved him so very much. Because he made us feel holy. And he made us feel whole. He made us feel loved. And he made us feel that we were worth something finally on this planet Earth. Finally we had some worth."[158]

Gradually, however, Malcolm came to reject some of the philosophy of the Nation of Islam, including its insistence that whites were "devils" and that blacks should live separately from them. In March 1964 he quit the group to begin the Muslim Mosque, a new black Muslim group, and soon began creating the Organization of Afro-American Unity (OAAU). A statement of purpose that he approved for the group in early 1965 was one of the decade's ultimate declarations of black pride: "We assert that Afro-Americans have the right to direct and control our lives, our history and our future rather than to have our destiny determined by American racists. . . . And thereby to again become a free people."[159] Malcolm's split with the Nation of Islam was a bitter one. When he was shot to death on February 21, 1965, while giving a speech in New York, it was believed he had been assassinated by the Black Muslims he once helped lead.

African and American

Malcolm also popularized a cultural movement that awakened a new sense of respect in many blacks for their past and their ancestors. Like many other blacks, Malcolm believed they should learn about their African heritage, which had been stolen from them when they were brought to America as slaves: "We are determined to rediscover our true African culture which was crushed and hidden for over four hundred years in order to enslave us."[160]

Although Malcolm did a great deal to foster pride in black heritage, he was not the first black to do so. As early as 1961, John Henrik Clarke of New York had expressed the same thought in the fall edition of *Freedomways* magazine:

We must Africanize everything! Our names, our manners and customs. Begin with yourself today. You have nothing to lose or fear. It is as natural for persons of African descent to take and maintain the customs, dress and traditions of their motherland, as it is natural for people of European descent to continue European customs and traditions in America. Our liberation must be complete. Support Africanization![161]

Gradually through the decade, blacks began to embrace their African roots. Both men and women wore flowing shirts called dashikis, Afro hairstyles, and African-styled jewelry. And just as Malcolm had changed his last name to "X" because "Little" was a reminder of his ancestors' slavery, many other blacks adopted African names. Stokely Carmichael became Kwame Ture and boxer Cassius Clay switched to Muhammad Ali. Theresa Jordan, an eighth grade student in New York City, got rid of her "slave name" and took the first name "Karriema" instead: "One was just as good as the other, as long as it was African,"[162] said Jordan.

Blacks began demanding that the general terms that whites then used to refer to them—"Negro" and the more demeaning "colored"—also be changed. As early as 1960 Richard B. Moore had written that a new name was needed:

> The important thing about a name is the impression which it makes in the minds of others and the reactions which it involves through the operation of the association of ideas. The purpose of the name "Negro" was to mark this people by virtue of their color for a special condition of oppression, degradation, exploitation, and annihilation.[163]

As an alternative, Moore suggested "Afri-American." Although Moore's alternative never caught on, Negroes in the 1960s embraced the term "black," with "African American" becoming as popular in later years. In a 1968 speech at Syracuse University, CORE's James Farmer said the switch to black was ironic: "Black Americans began asserting their blackness as never before. Ten years ago, fifteen years ago if you called a man black it would have been a fighting word, because he thought black was evil [but] now he would assert, 'I am a black man.'"[164]

The appreciation blacks now felt for their heritage created a fierce desire to learn more about their past. The result was a drive for black studies programs that sparked battles as bitter as any civil rights struggle in the South.

Black Studies

In the 1968–1969 school year at Cornell University in Ithaca, New York, there were only 250 black students out of an enrollment of over 14,000. In a series of protests, those black students forcefully demanded that the school create classes on their African heritage and on the experience of blacks throughout American history. The students staged a sit-in at the office of President James A. Perkins, overturned furniture in two administration buildings, and engaged in other disruptive activities.

Even after schools agreed to start such programs, many black students continued protesting because they did not like the choice of subjects offered or disagreed with the people chosen as instructors; many blacks, for example, believed that only black instructors should be hired for such programs. Perkins once tried to explain why he believed students became so militant in their demands:

> The problem we did not foresee when we started this [black studies] program is the problem the country did not foresee, that is, the problems that have arisen out of the great drive for Negro identity [and] out of growing militancy. These came with the increase in numbers [of black students]. As soon as black students were numerous enough here, they no longer felt themselves a lost people. They did not wish to lose themselves in the largely white student body, so they decided to combine.[165]

That analysis applied not only to Cornell but to other schools across the nation.

Black students were no longer content to be just campus curiosities. They wanted themselves and their heritage to be respected, and black studies programs were the remedy. The academic demands were simply a flexing of the power that blacks now had.

One of the first black studies programs started in 1963 at Merritt Junior College in Oakland, California, at the request of Huey Newton, who four years later would found the Black Panther Party with fellow student Bobby Seale. Although school administrators agreed to implement the one class, Newton was upset when the course was titled "Negro History" and taught by a white. "The cat that was teaching it didn't know what he was

Malcolm X Rejects Racism

In April 1964, Malcolm X made a religious pilgrimage called a hajj to Mecca, the Muslim holy city. He also visited many African and Middle Eastern countries and met other Muslims from around the world. The trip changed Malcolm because he came into contact with Muslims who, although they were white, accepted black Muslims as their equals. Malcolm was so deeply affected by this acceptance that he came to believe that whites did not have to be enemies of blacks. In letters he wrote during the trip, Malcolm said he no longer hated whites, as dictated by Nation of Islam leader Elijah Muhammad. His words are taken from A Documentary History of the Negro People in the United States 1960–1968, *edited by Herbert Aptheker.*

The whites as well as nonwhites who accept true Islam become a changed people. I have eaten from the same plate with people whose eyes were the bluest of blue, whose hair was the blondest of blond, and whose skin was the whitest of white—all the way from Cairo to Jedda and even in the Holy City of Mecca itself—and I felt the same sincerity in the words and deeds of these "white" Muslims that I felt among the African Muslims of Nigeria, Sudan, and Ghana. . . . I declare emphatically that I am no longer in Elijah Muhammad's "strait jacket," and I don't intend to replace his with one woven by someone else. I am a Muslim. This religion recognizes all men as brothers. It accepts all human beings as equal before God, and as equal members in the Human Family of Mankind. I totally reject Elijah Muhammad's racist philosophy, which he has labeled "Islam" only to fool and misuse gullible people, as he fooled and misused me.

teaching. He really wasn't teaching Black History; he was teaching American history and reiterating slavery,"[166] complained Newton, who refused to take the course.

By the late sixties, black students on college campuses across America were demanding courses on African history and culture as well as the history of blacks in America. And they knew exactly the kind of courses they wanted to take. James Turner, a Northwestern University student who in 1968 led a takeover of administration offices during a black studies protest, said the students themselves had the right to create black studies curricula: "Why is Latin more relevant than Swahili, Hausa or Arabic? Latin is a dead language. The people who can best judge these things, I believe, are the people most related to the problem, namely, black people."[167]

To force schools to offer such courses, students protested with rallies, marches, and sit-ins, demonstrations that sometimes became violent. Beginning in 1965, San Francisco State University went through several years of turmoil when the Black Students Union (BSU) led a series of protests. In the fall of 1967, members of the BSU invaded the offices of the campus newspaper and beat up its editor for allegedly making insulting remarks about blacks. When some students were suspended in the incident, a BSU demonstration was followed by an attempt to burn down a campus bookstore.

Violence also occurred in 1969 at the University of California–Los Angeles (UCLA) when members of US, a militant group founded by Ron Karenga, and the Black Panthers fought over who would direct UCLA's Afro-American Studies Center. The arguments led to a shooting on January 17, 1969, that killed Panthers John Huggins and Alprentice Carter. Three members of US were convicted in the slayings.

Black Electoral Victories

While growing self-confidence led black students to reshape higher education, other blacks were making even more important changes in American life. With the victories black candidates were winning at the ballot box, they could revolutionize politics.

The federal Voting Rights Act of 1965 provided, for the first time, direct federal intervention to enable blacks to register and vote. Between 1965 and 1970, more than a million new black voters registered in southern states. In that same period the number of blacks holding elective office in the South rose from fewer than one hundred to more than six hundred. One of the new officials in 1969 was Maynard Jackson, who was elected to the Atlanta city council with three other blacks. Four years later, Jackson became that city's first black mayor.

Although blacks had always been able to vote in the North, many had never bothered to take part in elections. But now black ballot power began to be felt as never before because the number of black voters was growing and more blacks than ever

Cassius Clay to Muhammad Ali

One of the most famous and beloved sports figures of the sixties was boxer Muhammad Ali. He won worldwide recognition as Cassius Clay when he won a gold medal in boxing for the United States at the 1960 Summer Olympics and captured the heavyweight world championship on February 25, 1964. But the day after he became world champion, Clay changed his name to Muhammad Ali, creating a furor not only in sports but the world at large. Ali also created controversy in 1967 when he refused to be drafted into the U.S. Army on religious grounds because he was a member of the Nation of Islam. In Hampton and Fayer's Voices of Freedom: An Oral History of the Civil Rights Movement from the 1950s Through the 1980s, *Ali explains that he changed his name because he believed he was a symbol to other blacks.*

A black man said, "I am the greatest." We weren't taught like that. We were taught the black man had the bad luck. Black was bad and white was good. So me, being black—"I am the greatest. I'm pretty"—it gave more [black] people confidence and it put me in such a spot. I had to fight to back up my words. It's a superior attitude. This made me so hated by many of the southerners, whites and blacks. This is confidence and character and different. That's what made me so popular. I liked being who I was because they would put me on television and when I say, "I'm the greatest. I'm pretty," that means little black children and people who felt like nothing say, "We got a champion. Look what he's doing. Look at him over there."

Cassius Clay shocked the world when he changed his name to Muhammad Ali in 1964.

were casting ballots without fear of violence. In 1967 Carl Stokes was elected mayor of Cleveland, Ohio, becoming the first black to run a major city. In the election he had an unlikely ally—the Black Panthers. Panther Jimmy Slater explains how the party helped Stokes: "We passed flyers out, went door-to-door. We registered people to vote for Stokes. We went throughout the community, registering people to vote, and passed out literature and leaflets at churches. A lot of [Panthers] worked at campaign headquarters."[168]

To ensure they would win enough white votes, black candidates like Stokes had to delicately address racial issues. In his autobiography, Stokes explains that he asked Martin Luther King not to stage any protests in Cleveland during the election because black protests might alienate white voters that Stokes needed to win. King agreed, but Stokes admits it had been difficult to make such a request of a civil rights legend: "It was a confrontation with a man whose recorded words I turn to for solace and inspiration at times of depression. But it came down to the hard game of politics—whether we wanted a cause or a victory. I wanted to win. Our people needed me to win."[169]

During the decade more blacks also began winning election to Congress, including Edward W. Brooke, a Massachusetts senator. And those black elected officials now had power—real power—to change the way blacks would be treated in the future.

Black Renaissance

The decade of the sixties was a period of great change for blacks. In a 1968 speech that year at Syracuse University, CORE's James Farmer claimed it was a wonderful time:

I believe that we are in a period that will be seen by historians as a period of the black renaissance. A period when the black man is seeking to find himself; when critical discussion and debate in the black community will reach its height; when there will be a flourishing of art and creative writing; when the black man will suddenly come alive. He will find an identity, not merely an answer to that age old question, "Who am I?" but more significantly, an answer to the question, "What is my relationship to society and to the people round about me?"[170]

That black renaissance and the search for an answer to that second, more profound question continue even today.

Notes

Introduction: A Decade of Revolt Against Racism

1. Quoted in Herbert Aptheker, ed., *A Documentary History of the Negro People in the United States 1960–1968*, vol. 7, *From the Alabama Protests to the Death of Martin Luther King, Jr.* New York: Carol, 1994, p. 196.

2. Quoted in Henry Hampton and Steve Fayer, *Voices of Freedom: An Oral History of the Civil Rights Movement from the 1950s Through the 1980s.* New York: Bantam Books, 1990, p. 19.

3. Quoted in Douglas Brinkley, *Rosa Parks.* New York: Penguin Putnam, 2000, p. 110.

4. Quoted in Brinkley, *Rosa Parks*, p. 3.

Chapter 1: Preacher Power: Black Ministers Lead the Fight

5. Quoted in Howell Raines, *My Soul Is Rested: Movement Days in the Deep South Remembered.* New York: Penguin Books, 1983, p. 69.

6. Quoted in Fred Powledge, *Free at Last: The Civil Rights Movement and the People Who Made It.* Boston: Little, Brown, 1990, p. 200.

7. Quoted in Raines, *My Soul Is Rested*, p. 70.

8. Quoted in David Levering Lewis, *King: A Biography.* Chicago: University of Illinois Press, 1978, p. 12.

9. Quoted in William Roger Witherspoon, *Martin Luther King: To the Mountaintop.* Garden City, NY: Doubleday, 1985, p. 4.

10. Quoted in Witherspoon, *Martin Luther King*, p. 13.

11. Quoted in Anthony Lewis and the *New York Times, Portrait of a Decade: The Second American Revolution.* New York: Random House, 1964, p. 70.

12. Quoted in Thomas R. Brooks, *Walls Come Tumbling Down: A History of the Civil Rights Movement 1940–1970.* Englewood Cliffs, NJ: Prentice-Hall, 1974, p. 138.

13. Raines, *My Soul Is Rested*, p. 69.

14. Quoted in Andrew M. Manis, *A Fire You Can't Put Out: The Civil Rights Life of Birmingham's Reverend Fred Shuttlesworth.* Tuscaloosa: University of Alabama Press, 1999, p. 155.

15. Quoted in Powledge, *Free at Last*, p. 80.

16. Quoted in Manis, *Fire You Can't Put Out*, p. 378.
17. Quoted in Manis, *Fire You Can't Put Out*, p. 378.
18. Quoted in Juan Williams, *Eyes on the Prize: America's Civil Rights Years, 1954–1965*. New York: Viking Penguin, 1987, p. 264.
19. Quoted in Williams, *Eyes on the Prize*, p. 265.
20. Quoted in Raines, *My Soul Is Rested*, p. 223.
21. Quoted in Aldon D. Morris, *The Origins of the Civil Rights Movement: Black Communities Organizing for Change*. New York: Free Press, 1984, p. 225.
22. Quoted in Powledge, *Free at Last*, p. 505.
23. Quoted in Hampton and Fayer, *Voices of Freedom*, p. 238.
24. Quoted in Dick J. Reavis, *If White Kids Die*. Denton: University of North Texas Press, 2001, p. 33.
25. Quoted in Williams, *Eyes on the Prize*, p. 268.
26. Quoted in Morris, *The Origins of the Civil Rights Movement*, pp. 261–62.

Chapter 2: Sit-Ins: Young People Fight for Their Rights

27. Quoted in Brooks, *Walls Come Tumbling Down*, p. 146.
28. Quoted in Williams, *Eyes on the Prize*, p. 127.
29. Quoted in Raines, *My Soul Is Rested*, p. 80.
30. Quoted in Morris, *The Origins of the Civil Rights Movement*, p. 202.
31. Quoted in Morris, *The Origins of the Civil Rights Movement*, p. 208.
32. Quoted in Morris, *The Origins of the Civil Rights Movement*, p. 201.
33. Quoted in August Meier, Elliott Rudwick, and Francis L. Broderick, eds., *Black Protest Thought in the Twentieth Century*. New York: Bobbs-Merrill, 1971, p. 309.
34. Quoted in Howard Zinn, *SNCC: The New Abolitionists*. Boston: Beacon Press, 1965, p. 7.
35. Quoted in Robert H. Brisbane, *Black Activism: Racial Revolution in the United States 1954–1970*. Valley Forge, PA: Judson Press, 1974, p. 47.
36. Quoted in Powledge, *Free at Last*, p. 235.
37. Quoted in Powledge, *Free at Last*, p. 235.
38. Quoted in Aptheker, *Documentary History of the Negro People*, p. 14.
39. Quoted in Williams, *Eyes on the Prize*, p. 132.
40. Quoted in Powledge, *Free at Last*, p. 209.
41. Quoted in Zinn, *SNCC*, p. 39.
42. Quoted in John Dittmer, *Local People: The Struggle for Civil Rights in Mississippi*. Chicago: University of Illinois Press, 1994, p. 87.

43. Quoted in Leon Friedman, ed., *The Civil Rights Reader: Basic Documents of the Civil Rights Movement*. New York: Walker, 1968, p. 47.
44. Quoted in Zinn, *SNCC*, p. 17.
45. Quoted in Aptheker, *Documentary History of the Negro People*, p. 18.
46. Quoted in Dittmer, *Local People*, p. 86.
47. Quoted in Brisbane, *Black Activism*, p. 49.
48. Quoted in Hampton and Fayer, *Voices of Freedom*, p. 66.
49. Quoted in Williams, *Eyes on the Prize*, p. 139.
50. Quoted in Williams, *Eyes on the Prize*, p. 121.

Chapter 3: Freedom Riders: Integrating Interstate Travel

51. Quoted in Clayborne Carson et al., eds., *The Eyes on the Prize Civil Rights Reader: Documents, Speeches, and Firsthand Accounts from the Black Freedom Struggle, 1954–1990*. New York: Viking, 1991, p. 125.
52. James Peck, *Freedom Ride*. New York: Simon and Schuster, 1962, pp. 16–17.
53. Quoted in Brooks, *Walls Come Tumbling Down*, p. 160.
54. Quoted in Raines, *My Soul Is Rested*, p. 111.
55. Quoted in Hampton and Fayer, *Voices of Freedom*, p. 76.
56. Peck, *Freedom Ride*, p. 116.
57. Quoted in Raines, *My Soul Is Rested*, p. 115.
58. Peck, *Freedom Ride*, p. 129.
59. Quoted in Morris, *The Origins of the Civil Rights Movement*, p. 232.
60. Quoted in Williams, *Eyes on the Prize*, p. 149.
61. Quoted in Hampton and Fayer, *Voices of Freedom*, p. 86.
62. Quoted in Williams, *Eyes on the Prize*, p. 154.
63. Quoted in Zinn, *SNCC*, p. 48.
64. Quoted in Lewis, *King*, p. 133.
65. Quoted in Williams, *Eyes on the Prize*, p. 159.
66. Quoted in *Peoria Journal*, "Changing the Nation," October 24, 1999. www.pjstar.com.
67. Quoted in Hampton and Fayer, *Voices of Freedom*, p. 94.
68. Quoted in Carson et al., *Eyes on the Prize Civil Rights Reader*, p. 126.
69. Quoted in *Peoria Journal*.
70. Quoted in Zinn, *SNCC*, p. 57.
71. Quoted in Raines, *My Soul Is Rested*, p. 102.

Chapter 4: Voter Registration: The Fight for the Right to Vote

72. Quoted in Brooks, *Walls Come Tumbling Down*, p. 171.
73. Quoted in Lewis, *King*, p. 93.
74. Quoted in Lewis and *New York Times, Portrait of a Decade*, p. 137.
75. Quoted in Hampton and Fayer, *Voices of Freedom*, p. 141.

76. Quoted in Hampton and Fayer, *Voices of Freedom*, p. 140.

77. Quoted in Carson et al., *Eyes on the Prize Civil Rights Reader*, p. 170.

78. Quoted in Morris, *The Origins of the Civil Rights Movement*, p. 240.

79. Quoted in Herb Boyd, ed., *Autobiography of a People: Three Centuries of African-American History Told by Those Who Lived It*. New York: Doubleday, 2000, p. 196.

80. Quoted in Morris, *The Origins of the Civil Rights Movement*, p. 238.

81. Quoted in Dittmer, *Local People*, p. 71.

82. Quoted in Raines, *My Soul Is Rested*, p. 242.

83. Quoted in Brisbane, *Black Activism*, p. 76.

84. Quoted in Brisbane, *Black Activism*, p. 77.

85. Quoted in Carson et al., *Eyes on the Prize Civil Rights Reader*, p. 174.

86. Quoted in Dittmer, *Local People*, p. 104.

87. Quoted in University of Southern Mississippi (USM) Libraries and USM's Center for Oral History and Cultural Heritage, An Oral History with Fannie Lou Hamer. www.lib.usm.edu.

88. Quoted in Hampton and Fayer, *Voices of Freedom*, p. 251.

89. Quoted in Raines, *My Soul Is Rested*, p. 275.

90. Quoted in Hampton and Fayer, *Voices of Freedom*, p. 193.

91. Quoted in Cheryl Lynn Greenberg, *A Circle of Trust: Remembering SNCC*. New Brunswick, NJ: Rutgers University Press, 1998, p. 71.

92. Quoted in Debra L. Schultz, *Going South: Jewish Women in the Civil Rights Movement*. New York: New York University Press, 2001, p. 69.

93. Quoted in Lewis, *King*, p. 268.

94. Quoted in Ralph David Abernathy, *And the Walls Came Tumbling Down: Ralph David Abernathy: An Autobiography*. New York: Harper & Row, 1989, p. 321.

95. Quoted in University of Southern Mississippi, Oral History with Fannie Lou Hamer.

96. Quoted in Dittmer, *Local People*, p. 242.

Chapter 5: Black Power: A New Militancy for Blacks

97. Martin Luther King Jr., "I Have a Dream." www.creighton.edu.

98. Quoted in Brisbane, *Black Activism*, p. 72.

99. Quoted in George R. Metcalf, *Black Profiles*. New York: McGraw-Hill, 1970, p. 351.

100. Quoted in Lewis V. Baldwin, *To Make the Wounded Whole: The Cultural Legacy of Martin Luther King, Jr*. Minneapolis: Fortress

Press, 1992, p. 30.

101. Quoted in Meier, Rudwick, and Broderick, *Black Protest Thought in the Twentieth Century*, p. 469.

102. Quoted in Morris, *The Origins of the Civil Rights Movement*, p. 164.

103. Quoted in Carson et al., *Eyes on the Prize Civil Rights Reader*, p. 112.

104. Quoted in Boyd, *Autobiography of a People*, p. 403.

105. Quoted in Greenberg, *Circle of Trust*, p. 169.

106. Quoted in Frontline, "The Two Nations of Black America," Public Broadcasting System, February 10, 1998. www.pbs.org.

107. Quoted in August Meier, Elliott Rudwick, and John Bracey Jr., eds., *Black Protest in the Sixties: Articles from the* New York Times. New York: Markus Wiener, 1991, p. 141.

108. Quoted in Meier, Rudwick, and Bracey, *Black Protest in the Sixties*, p. 141.

109. Quoted in Carson et al., *Eyes on the Prize Civil Rights Reader*, p. 281.

110. Quoted in Adam Fairclough, *To Redeem the Soul of America: The Southern Christian Leadership Conference and Martin Luther King, Jr.* Athens: University of Georgia Press, 1987, p. 316.

111. Quoted in Brisbane, *Black Activism*, p. 141.

112. Quoted in Hampton and Fayer, *Voices of Freedom*, p. 290.

113. Quoted in Charles E. Jones, ed., *The Black Panther Party (Reconsidered)*. Baltimore: Black Classic Press, 1998, p. 159.

114. Quoted in Metcalf, *Black Profiles*, p. 381.

115. Quoted in Metcalf, *Black Profiles*, p. 381.

116. Quoted in Jones, *The Black Panther Party*, p. 31.

117. Quoted in Witherspoon, *Martin Luther King*, p. 162.

118. Quoted in Hampton and Fayer, *Voices of Freedom*, p. 376.

119. Quoted in Hampton and Fayer, *Voices of Freedom*, p. 379.

120. Quoted in Lewis, *King*, p. 381.

121. Quoted in Abernathy, *And the Walls Came Tumbling Down*, p. 418.

122. Quoted in Abernathy, *And the Walls Came Tumbling Down*, p. 418.

123. Quoted in Baldwin, *To Make the Wounded Whole*, p. 219.

124. Quoted in MLK Online, "Martin Luther King, Jr." www.mlkonline.com.

Chapter 6: White Backlash: Resisting the Civil Rights Movement

125. Quoted in Lewis and *New York Times, Portrait of a Decade*, p. 185.

126. Quoted in Powledge, *Free at Last*, p. 146.

127. Quoted in Michael Newton, *The Invisible Empire: The Ku Klux Klan in Florida*. Gainesville:

University Press of Florida, 2001, p. 176.

128. Quoted in Greenberg, *A Circle of Trust*, p. 68.

129. Quoted in Williams, *Eyes on the Prize*, p. 194.

130. Quoted in Raines, *My Soul Is Rested*, p. 106.

131. Quoted in Patsy Sims, *The Klan*. Lexington: University Press of Kentucky, 1996, p. 199.

132. Quoted in Stephan Lesher, *George Wallace: American Populist*. New York: Addison, 1994, p. 148.

133. Quoted in Lewis, *King*, p. 196.

134. Quoted in Greenberg, *A Circle of Trust*, p. 60.

135. Quoted in Sims, *Klan*, p. 210.

136. Quoted in Wyn Craig Wade, *The Fiery Cross: The Ku Klux Klan in America*. New York: Simon and Schuster, 1987, p. 321.

137. Quoted in Public Broadcasting System, "George Wallace: Settin' the Woods on Fire." www.pbs.org.

138. Quoted in Brooks, *Walls Come Tumbling Down*, p. 212.

139. Quoted in Raines, *My Soul Is Rested*, p. 33.

140. James Meredith, *Three Years in Mississippi*. Bloomington: Indiana University Press, 1966, p. 273.

141. Quoted in Williams, *Eyes on the Prize*, p. 215.

142. Meredith, *Three Years in Mississippi*, p. 211.

143. Quoted in Meredith, *Three Years in Mississippi*, p. 226.

144. Quoted in Bruce Galphin, *The Riddle of Lester Maddox*. Atlanta, GA: Camelot, 1968, p. 22.

145. Quoted in Galphin, *The Riddle of Lester Maddox*, p. 169.

146. Quoted in Hal Jacobs, "Lester! The Strange but True Tale of Georgia's Unlikeliest Governor," *Creative Loafing*, March 20, 1999. www.southerncurrents.com.

147. Quoted in Sims, *Klan*, p. 194.

148. Quoted in Public Broadcasting System, "George Wallace: Settin' the Woods on Fire."

Chapter 7: Black Pride: A New Mood Sweeps the Nation

149. Quoted in Meier, Rudwick, and Bracey, *Black Protest in the Sixties*, p. 4.

150. Quoted in Powledge, *Free at Last*, p. 22.

151. Quoted in Brooks, *Walls Come Tumbling Down*, p. 94.

152. Quoted in Meier, Rudwick, and Broderick, *Black Protest Thought in the Twentieth Century*, p. 573.

153. Quoted in Metcalf, *Black Profiles*, p. 341.

154. Quoted in Friedman, *The Civil Rights Reader*, p. 105.

155. Quoted in Meier, Rudwick, and Broderick, *Black Protest Thought in the Twentieth Century*, p. 388.

156. Quoted in Meier, Rudwick, and

Bracey, *Black Protest in the Sixties*, p. 40.

157. Quoted in Friedman, *The Civil Rights Reader*, p. 114.
158. Quoted in Hampton and Fayer, *Voices of Freedom*, p. 255.
159. Quoted in William L. Van Deburg, ed., *Modern Black Nationalism: From Marcus Garvey to Louis Farrakhan*. New York: New York University Press, 1997, p. 109.
160. Quoted in Van Deburg, *Modern Black Nationalism*, p. 109.
161. Quoted in Brisbane, *Black Activism*, p. 179.
162. Quoted in Carson et al., *The Eyes on the Prize Civil Rights Reader*, p. 377.
163. Quoted in Aptheker, *A Documentary History of the Negro People*, p. 10.
164. Quoted in Meier, Rudwick, and Broderick, *Black Protest Thought in the Twentieth Century*, p. 574.
165. Quoted in Meier, Rudwick, and Bracey, *Black Protest in the Sixties*, p. 247.
166. Quoted in Brisbane, *Black Activism*, p. 195.
167. Quoted in Meier, Rudwick, and Bracey, *Black Protest in the Sixties*, p. 254.
168. Quoted in Jones, *The Black Panther Party*, p. 150.
169. Quoted in Carson et al., *The Eyes on the Prize Civil Rights Reader*, p. 341.
170. Quoted in Meier, Rudwick, and Broderick, *Black Protest Thought in the Twentieth Century*, p. 570.

For Further Reading

Thomas R. Brooks, *Walls Come Tumbling Down: A History of the Civil Rights Movement 1940–1970.* Englewood Cliffs, NJ: Prentice-Hall, 1974. A comprehensive history of the fight for black rights in this period.

Henry Hampton and Steve Fayer, *Voices of Freedom: An Oral History of the Civil Rights Movement from the 1950s Through the 1980s.* New York: Bantam Books, 1990. An excellent book built around interviews with the men and women who fought for civil rights.

Martin Luther King Jr., *Stride Toward Freedom: The Montgomery Story.* New York: HarperCollins, 1986. King documents the bus boycott that launched the modern civil rights movement.

David Levering Lewis, *King: A Biography.* Chicago: University of Illinois Press, 1978. In one of the best biographies of King, Lewis offers a fascinating look at King's life.

Milton Meltzer, *The Black Americans: A History in Their Own Words 1619–1983.* New York: Thomas Y. Crowell, 1984. The historian relies extensively on speeches and writings of past black leaders to tell the story of the black experience.

James Meredith, *Three Years in Mississippi.* Bloomington: Indiana University Press, 1966. Meredith's firsthand account of what it was like to brave racism as a college student.

Patsy Sims, *The Klan.* Lexington: University Press of Kentucky, 1996. This excellent book on the Ku Klux Klan is based on interviews with Klan members and victims of Klan violence.

Juan Williams, *Eyes on the Prize: America's Civil Rights Years, 1954–1965.* New York: Viking Penguin, 1987. This companion book to the Public Broadcasting System television series of the same name is an excellent civil rights history. It also has wonderful pictures.

Howard Zinn, *SNCC: The New Abolitionists.* Boston: Beacon Press, 1965. The author, an adviser to the Student Nonviolent Coordinating Committee, brings an insider's knowledge to this history of the group.

Works Consulted

Books

Ralph David Abernathy, *And the Walls Came Tumbling Down: Ralph David Abernathy: An Autobiography.* New York: Harper & Row, 1989. Martin Luther King Jr.'s friend and top aide details his long civil rights career.

Herbert Aptheker, ed., *A Documentary History of the Negro People in the United States 1960–1968.* Vol. 7, *From the Alabama Protests to the Death of Martin Luther King, Jr.* New York: Carol, 1994. This collection of documents, interviews, speeches, and other works provides an interesting look at the civil rights movement in this period.

Lewis V. Baldwin, *To Make the Wounded Whole: The Cultural Legacy of Martin Luther King, Jr.* Minneapolis: Fortress Press, 1992. A scholarly book on how King's life influenced the development of blacks and American culture.

Herb Boyd, ed., *Autobiography of a People: Three Centuries of African-American History Told by Those Who Lived It.* New York: Doubleday, 2000. Includes firsthand accounts of what it was like for civil rights workers to battle racism.

Douglas Brinkley, *Rosa Parks.* New York: Penguin Putnam, 2000. A well-written biography of this famous civil rights heroine.

Robert H. Brisbane, *Black Activism: Racial Revolution in the United States 1954–1970.* Valley Forge, PA: Judson Press, 1974. The author provides a solid history of how blacks fought for their civil rights and the changes that took place in their methods.

Clayborne Carson et al., eds., *The Eyes on the Prize Civil Rights Reader: Documents, Speeches, and Firsthand Accounts from the Black Freedom Struggle, 1954–1990.* New York: Viking, 1991. This excellent collection contains information about what happened during the civil rights movement as well as why it happened.

John Dittmer, *Local People: The Struggle for Civil Rights in Mississippi.* Chicago: University of Illinois Press, 1994. The author explains how ordinary people fought for civil rights in one of the most racist states.

Adam Fairclough, *To Redeem the Soul of America: The Southern Christian Leadership Conference and Martin Luther King, Jr.* Athens: University of Georgia Press, 1987. A solid history of the SCLC that focuses on King, who helped create it and led it for over a decade.

Leon Friedman, ed., *The Civil Rights Reader: Basic Documents of the Civil Rights Movement*. New York: Walker, 1968. This collection of speeches, documents, and other sources provides interesting highlights about civil rights, including personal experiences of many of those involved in the fight.

Bruce Galphin, *The Riddle of Lester Maddox*. Atlanta, GA: Camelot, 1968. The author provides a comprehensive look at the life of this Georgia governor.

Cheryl Lynn Greenberg, *A Circle of Trust: Remembering SNCC*. New Brunswick, NJ: Rutgers University Press, 1998. When SNCC workers held a reunion in 1988, the author interviewed them about their experiences to provide a fine firsthand account of what they did.

Paul Hendrickson, *Sons of Mississippi*. New York: Alfred A. Knopf, 2003. An interesting look at not only James Meredith and other civil rights figures but some of the whites who opposed them.

Peter Irons, *The Courage of Their Convictions: Sixteen Americans Who Fought Their Way to the Supreme Court*. New York: Free Press, 1988. An interesting book that details high court cases important to history, including one involving a sit-in protester.

Charles E. Jones, ed., *The Black Panther Party (Reconsidered)*. Baltimore: Black Classic Press, 1998. This collection of essays offers an interesting look at the Black Panthers.

Stephan Lesher, *George Wallace: American Populist*. New York: Addison, 1994. A good biography of the Alabama governor.

Anthony Lewis and the *New York Times*, *Portrait of a Decade: The Second American Revolution*. New York: Random House, 1964. The book relies on *New York Times* stories to tell about the early battle for civil rights.

Andrew M. Manis, *A Fire You Can't Put Out: The Civil Rights Life of Birmingham's Reverend Fred Shuttlesworth*. Tuscaloosa: University of Alabama Press, 1999. A solid account of the work done by this renowned civil rights fighter.

August Meier, Elliott Rudwick, and Francis L. Broderick, eds., *Black Protest Thought in the Twentieth Century*. New York: Bobbs-Merrill, 1971. This collection of speeches and written works provides a detailed account of how blacks progressed through the twentieth century in trying to gain their rights.

August Meier, Elliott Rudwick, and John Bracey Jr., eds., *Black Protest in the Sixties: Articles from the* New York Times. New York: Markus Wiener, 1991. Fine stories from the newspaper's *Sunday* magazine that delve into the battle for civil rights in this decade.

George R. Metcalf, *Black Profiles.* New York: McGraw-Hill, 1970. The author details the lives of notable black leaders such as Malcolm X.

Aldon D. Morris, *The Origins of the Civil Rights Movement: Black Communities Organizing for Change.* New York: Free Press, 1984. An overview of the groups that fought for civil rights and how they interacted with each other during this turbulent period.

Michael Newton, *The Invisible Empire: The Ku Klux Klan in Florida.* Gainesville: University Press of Florida, 2001. An interesting look at how the KKK operated in this southern state.

James Peck, *Freedom Ride.* New York: Simon and Schuster, 1962. The author explains his experiences as a Freedom Rider, both in the 1940s and in 1961.

Fred Powledge, *Free at Last: The Civil Rights Movement and the People Who Made It.* Boston: Little, Brown, 1990. An interesting look at the fight for civil rights that focuses on the people involved.

Howell Raines, *My Soul Is Rested: Movement Days in the Deep South Remembered.* New York: Penguin Books, 1983. Through interviews with the men and women who did it, the author provides a fascinating look

at what it was like to work for civil rights in the sixties.

Dick J. Reavis, *If White Kids Die.* Denton: University of North Texas Press, 2001. The author recounts his days as a SNCC worker.

Debra L. Schultz, *Going South: Jewish Women in the Civil Rights Movement.* New York: New York University Press, 2001. The author interviewed Jewish women who volunteered as civil rights workers.

William L. Van Deburg, ed., *Modern Black Nationalism: From Marcus Garvey to Louis Farrakhan.* New York: New York University Press, 1997. Deburg uses the writings of historical black leaders to explain what black nationalism was and how it changed in the twentieth century.

Wyn Craig Wade, *The Fiery Cross: The Ku Klux Klan in America.* New York: Simon and Schuster, 1987. A solid book on the KKK that shows how it used violence to fight the civil rights movement.

William Roger Witherspoon, *Martin Luther King: To the Mountaintop.* Garden City, NY: Doubleday, 1985. A solid biography of King that includes many wonderful pictures that bring to life the civil rights leader and his era.

Internet Sources

Frontline, "The Two Nations of Black America," Public Broadcasting System, February 10, 1998. www.pbs.org.

Hal Jacobs, "Lester! The Strange but True Tale of Georgia's Unlikeliest Governor," *Creative Loafing*, March 20, 1999. www.southerncurrents.com.

Martin Luther King Jr., "I Have a Dream." www.creighton.edu.

———, "Letter From Birmingham Jail." www.creighton.edu.

MLK Online, "Martin Luther King, Jr." www.mlkonline.com.

Official Kwanzaa Website, Nguzo Saba (The Seven Principles). www.officialkwanzaawebsite.org.

Peoria Journal, "Changing the Nation," October 24, 1999. www.pjstar.com.

Public Broadcasting System, "George Wallace: Settin' the Woods on Fire." www.pbs.org.

University of Southern Mississippi (USM) Libraries and USM's Center for Oral History and Cultural Heritage, An Oral History with Fannie Lou Hamer. www.lib.usm.edu.

Marianne Worthington, "The Campaign Rhetoric of George Wallace in the 1968 Presidential Election," *The Upsilonian*, Summer 1992. www.cumber.edu.

Websites

The Civil Rights Movement (www.ecsu.ctstateu.edu). A useful list of many civil rights websites.

Greensboro Sit-ins: Launch of a Civil Rights Movement (www.sitins.com). Information, and pictures on sit-ins by the Greensboro (North Carolina) Public Library and *Greensboro News & Record* newspaper.

MLK Online (www.mlkonline.com). An Internet site dedicated to Martin Luther King Jr.

Veterans of the Civil Rights Movement (www.flightline.highline.edu). Highline Community College in Seattle, Washington, provides biographies and pictures of civil rights leaders.

Index

Abernathy, Ralph, 7–8, 14
A.C. Gaston Motel, 72
African Americans. See blacks
African heritage, 89–90
Afro hairstyle, 87, 90
Alabama Christian Movement for
    Human Rights (ACMHR), 14
Albany, Georgia, 49
Ali, Muhammad, 90, 93
Allen, Ivan, Jr., 64
Allen, Ralph, 49
Anderson, Candie, 29
Anniston, Alabama, 38, 40
arrests, 38, 39, 42, 44–45
    see also imprisonment
Atlanta, Georgia, 94

Baker, Ella, 25
Barnett, Ross, 80
Beckwith, Byron de la, 81
Bible, 11
Bigelow, Albert, 38
Biloxi, Mississippi, 31
Birmingham, Alabama
    bombings in, 19, 76
    Freedom Rides and, 44
    1963 marches through, 6
    violence by lawmen in, 15–16,
        62, 77
Black Is Beautiful, 87
Black Muslims. *See* Nation of Islam
black nationalism, 89
Black Panthers, 66–68, 92, 94

Black Power, 59–64, 65, 66, 87
black pride, 85–87, 88–90, 93
blacks
    elected officials, 94
    indignities suffered by, 7–8, 12,
        28, 85
    intimidation of, 46, 49, 50, 75,
        81–82
    self-image of
        inferiority, 84–87
        pride, 87, 88–90, 93
    use of term, 90
    wait by, for rights, 6–7, 21
Black Students Union (BSU), 92
black studies, 90–92, 94
Blackwell, Unita, 54
Blair, Ezell, Jr., 22
Bogalusa, Louisiana, 75
bombings
    of churches, 15, 62, 76
    of homes, 13, 15, 31, 72, 75
    KKK and, 75
    of SCLC headquarters, 19, 72
Bond, Julian, 63–64
Brooke, Edward W., 94
Brown v. Board of Education
    (1954), 37
bus boycotts, 9, 13

Carey, Gordon, 11
Carmichael, Stokely
    African name of, 90
    on assassination of King, 71

background of, 62
    black pride and, 87, 89
    in Parchman Prison, 45
    SNCC and, 63–66
Carter, Alprentice, 94
Caston, Billy Jack, 51
Chaney, James, 54–55
Chicago, Illinois, 68
Christian love, 30
churches, black, 10–11, 14, 20–21
Clark, Jim, 16–17
Clark, Obie, 78
Clarke, John Henrik, 89–90
Clay, Cassius, 90, 93
Cleage, Albert B. Jr., 59
Cleaver, Eldridge, 9, 66, 68, 89
Cleveland, Ohio, 94
Collins, Addie Mae, 76
Concerned White Citizens of
    Alabama, 19
Congress of Racial Equality
    (CORE)
    black churches and, 11
    Freedom Rides and, 36, 40
    Journey of Reconciliation and, 35
    riots in Harlem and, 68
    use of nonviolence and, 26
    voter registration drives and, 47, 54
conk hairstyle, 85
Connor, Eugene "Bull," 40, 62, 77
Cornell University, 90–92
Cotton, Dorothy, 50
Council of Federated
    Organizations (COFO), 52, 54

Cowling, Ell, 38
Craig, Calvin, 75
Cross, John, 20–21
Curry, Connie, 75
Cutrer, Jesse H., Jr., 75

Dawley, David, 66
Deacons for Defense and Justice, 69
Deep South, 35–36, 37
Dennis, Dave, 54
Detroit, Michigan, 68, 69–70
Dowdy, June, 46
Du Bois, W.E.B., 84

education
    of black ministers, 10
    black studies and, 90–92, 94
    integration of, 37, 73, 79–82
Ellis, Talbott, 6
Ellwanger, Joseph, 19–20
Evers, Medgar, 62, 81

Farmer, James
    on black renaissance, 94–95
    on black self-image, 85, 86
    Freedom Rides, 36–37, 42
    on use of term blacks, 90
Federal Bureau of Investigation
    (FBI), 68
Fellowship of Reconciliation
    (FOR), 26, 35
Florida Agricultural and Mining
    College, 27
Folks, Warren, 74
Freedom Ride (Peck), 35–36
Freedom Rides
    arrests during, 38, 39, 42, 44–45
    background of, 35–36
    fear of participants in, 34–35, 37
    strategy of, 36–38

success of, 45
    violence during, 38–39, 40,
        41–42, 43, 77
Freedom Summer, 52, 54–56
Freedomways (magazine), 89–90
F.W.Woolworth Company stores,
    22, 23, 24, 27

Gandhi, Mohandas (Mahatma), 26,
    30
Gaston Hotel, 19
Gober, Bertha, 39, 57
Goodman, Andrew, 54–55
Gordon, Bob, 19
Grant, Joanne, 54
Greensboro, North Carolina, 22,
    31–33
Greyhound buses. See Freedom Rides
Guihard, Paul, 80
Gunn, Roy, 78
Gunter, Ray, 80
Guyot, Lawrence, 50

Hamer, Fannie Lou, 52, 53, 57
Harlem, New York, 68
Hillard, David, 68
Hood, James A., 79–80
Huggins, John, 94
Hunt, Frank, 34
Hurst, F.H., 51, 56

"I Have a Dream" (King), 58, 59
imprisonment
    of Freedom Riders, 45
    of King, 15
    of protesters, 29
    of voter registration drive work-
        ers, 51
integration
    of education, 37, 73, 79–82

of public facilities
    eating establishments, 22–25,
        27–28, 29, 31–33, 82–83
    libraries, 28–29
    transportation, 45
    refusal to accept, by state officials,
        72–73, 75, 77, 78–80, 82
Interstate Commerce Commission
    (ICC), 45
Invaders, 70–71

Jackson, Maynard, 94
Jackson, Mississippi, 28–29, 42, 45
jailings. See imprisonment
Jenkins, Herbert, 64–65
Jennings, Regina, 67
Jim Crow, 7, 33
Johnson, Lyndon B., 57
Jones, Charles, 84–85
Jordan, Theresa, 90
Journey of Reconciliation, 35–36

Karenga, Ron, 92
Kasen, Allen, 41
Kennedy, John F.
    Freedom Rides and, 37, 42
    integration and, 45, 79, 80
Kennedy, Robert F., 37, 42
King, A.D. (Alfred Daniel), 21, 72
King, Coretta Scott, 13, 14
King, Martin Luther, Jr.
    assassination of, 71
    background of, 12–13
    bombing of home and, 13
    Freedom Rides and, 42
    importance of, 12, 24–25
    jailing of, 15
    on justice delayed, 21
    media coverage and, 18
    Montgomery bus boycott and, 9

on nonviolence, 13, 30, 71
on obligation to fight for civil
   rights, 13
on power of law, 42
on riot in Harlem, 68
on riot in Memphis, 71
on segregation, 13
SNCC and, 25
Stokes and, 94
on voting, 46–47, 56
King, Martin Luther, Sr., 12
King, Yolanda, 13
Klan, The (Patsy Sims), 83
Klantown, USA, 75
Kress stores, 24
Ku Klux Klan (KKK)
  beliefs of, 74, 77, 83
  Freedom Rides and, 38, 44
  government officials and, 75, 77,
    78
  informants within, 78
  violence by, 74–75

Lafayette, Bernard, 26–27, 41, 44
lawmen
  racism of, 75, 77–78
  as sympathizers, 78
  violence by
    in Birmingham, 15–16, 62, 77
    in Jackson, 29
    in Sasser, 77–78
    in Selma, 17
Lawson, James, 24–26
Lawson, Jim, 71
Lee, Bernard, 68
Lee, Herbert, 51, 56
Leonard, Frederick, 41, 42, 44
Lester, Julius, 61
"Letter from Birmingham Jail"
  (King), 15, 21

Lewis, John, 37, 38, 41, 42
Liberation (magazine), 62
Life (magazine), 74
Lillard, Leo, 33
literacy tests, 50
Little, Earl, 87
Little, Malcolm. *See* Malcolm X
Little, Philbert, 87
Loober, Z. Alexander, 31
Lowery, Joseph E.
  on black preachers, 10–11
  on religious base of SCLC, 12
  on support of SCLC by black
    churches, 14
  on Wallace, 17
Lynch, Connie, 76

Maddox, Lester, 82–83
Mahoney, William, 34–35, 45
Malcolm X
  on African heritage, 89
  assassination of, 89
  background of, 87–88
  Black Panthers and, 66
  black pride and, 88–89
  on black self-image, 85, 87
  on King, 61
  on March on Washington, 59
  rejects nonviolence, 59–61, 62, 63
  rejects racism, 89, 91
Malone, Vivian, 79–80
March on Washington (1963),
  58–59
Marshall, Thurgood, 85
Mason, Gilbert, 31
Mathews, Z.T., 49
McCain, Franklin, 22, 23, 24
McClellan stores, 24
McComb, Mississippi, 47
McDew, Charles, 74–75

McNair, Denise, 76
McNeil, Joseph, 22
media coverage
  of attempted integration of
    library, 29
  black image and, 85
  of King, 18
  of sit-ins, 23
  of violence in Selma, 17, 57
  of voter registration drives, 54
Memphis, Tennessee, 70–71
Meredith, James, 64, 80–82
Merritt Junior College, 92
militancy 59–64, 92
militant groups
  Black Panthers, 66, 68
  Invaders, 70–71
  SNCC, 63–66
  US, 92, 94
ministers
  black
    importance of, 10–11
    opposed to protests, 18
    power of, 20–21
    use of Bible by, 11
    voter registration and, 46
    white, 19–20, 44, 76
Montgomery, Alabama
  bus boycott in, 9, 13
  Freedom Rides in, 41
  march from Selma to, 18
Montgomery Advertiser (newspa-
  per), 30
Moody, Anne, 50
Moore, Amzie, 47
Moore, Richard B., 90
Moses, Robert, 47, 51–52, 54, 56
Muhammad, Elijah, 87, 91
murders
  during bombings, 76

of Evers, 62, 81
of Herbert Lee, 51, 56
of Malcolm X, 89
of Martin Luther King Jr., 71
during voter registration drives,
51, 54–55, 56
Muslim Mosque, 89

Nash, Diane, 28, 31–32, 40
Nashville, Tennessee, 24
National Association for the
Advancement of Colored People
(NAACP), 47, 61
National Guard
Detroit riots and, 70
Freedom Rides and, 34, 42
integration of universities and,
79, 80
Nation of Islam, 62, 87, 89, 91
Negroes. *See* blacks
Newark, New Jersey, 68
news coverage. *See* media coverage
Newton, Huey, 66, 68, 92
New York Times (newspaper), 47, 49
nonviolent resistance
importance of, 61
King and, 13
organizations using, 14, 26
philosophy of, 30, 71
rejected by
Black Panthers, 66, 68
blacks, 68–71
Malcolm X, 59–61, 62, 63
SNCC, 63–66
training in, 26–27, 37
North Carolina Agricultural and
Technical College, 22

Organization of Afro-American
Unity (OAAU), 89

Parchman Prison, 45
Parham, Grosbeck Preer, 6
Parks, Rosa, 9
Patterson, John, 41, 42, 73, 78
Peck, James, 35–36, 37, 40
Perkins, James, 38
Person, Charles, 37, 40
Pickrick Restaurant, 82–83
Porter, John, 21
preachers, black. *See* ministers, black
Price, Cecil, 54–55
Pritchett, Laurie, 39
public facilities. *See* integration, of
public facilities

racism
in Deep South, 35–36, 37
effects of, 7–8, 12, 13, 28, 84–87
of government officials, 75, 77–78
morality and, 32
Rainey, Lawrence, 55
Ray, James Earl, 71
Reagon, Cordell, 25, 49–50
religion
as basis for nonviolent resistance,
30
see also ministers
Rice, Daddy, 7
Richmond, David, 22
Richmond News Leader (newspaper), 31
riots, 68–71
Robertson, Carol, 76
Rodman, Edward, 29

Sanchez, Sonia, 89
San Francisco State University, 92
sanitation workers strike, 70–71
Sasser, Georgia, 49, 77–78
Schwarzchild, Henry, 32

Schwarzchild, Kathy, 32
Schwerner, Michael, 54–55
Schwerner, Rita, 54, 55
Scott, Coretta. *See* King, Coretta
Scott
Scott, Ron, 69
Seale, Bobby, 66, 68, 92
segregation
conditions of, 7–8, 9, 28, 34
in Deep South, 35–36
Seigenthaler, John, 41, 42, 43
self-defense, 61–62, 69
Selma, Alabama, 16–17, 18, 56–57
separate but equal, 34
Shelton, Robert, 75, 83
Sherrod, Charles, 49
Shuttlesworth, Fred L.
background of, 14
bombing of home and, 15
formation of SCLC and, 13–14
Freedom Rides and, 39–40
importance of, 21
injury of, 16, 77
on nonviolence resistance, 61
Sims, Charles R., 69
Sims, Patsy, 83
sit-ins, 22–25, 27–28, 29, 31–33
Sitton, Claude, 49
Sixteenth Street Baptist Church,
62, 76
Slater, Jimmy, 94
Smith, Howard K., 14
Smith, Kelly Miller, 11, 25
Smith, Nelson, 21
Smith, Ruby Doris, 42
Soul on Ice (Cleaver), 9
Souls of Black Folk (Du Bois), 84
Southern Christian Leadership
Conference (SCLC)
bombing of headquarters and,
19, 72

formation of, 11, 13–14
Freedom Rides and, 40
King and, 12
religious base of, 12, 14
services provided by, 17–18
voter registration drives and, 47
Steele, Charles K., 13–14
Stembridge, Jane, 26, 28
Stephens, Patricia, 27
Stokes, Carl, 94
Student Nonviolent Coordinating
   Committee (SNCC)
formation of, 25
Freedom Rides and, 40
KKK and, 74–75
militancy and, 63–66
voter registration drives and,
   47–52
whites excluded from, 66
Sullivan, L.B., 42
Supreme Court, 37, 45

Taylor, Lana, 28
television. *See* media coverage
Thelwell, Michael, 81
Thomas, Hank, 39
Three Years in Mississippi
   (Meredith), 80
Tougaloo Nine, 29
Trailways buses. *See* Freedom Rides
transportation, 9, 34
Ture, Kwame, 90
Turner, James, 92

University of Alabama, 79–80
University of California at Los
   Angeles, 92
University of Mississippi, 80–82
US (militant group), 92, 94

violence
  by blacks
    assassination of Malcolm X, 89
    by Black Panthers, 68
    over black studies, 92, 94
    reacting to whites, 29
    riots, 68–71
  media coverage and, 17, 57
  nonviolent response to, 26–27
  by whites
    during Freedom Rides, 38–40,
      41–42, 43, 77
    during integration of University
      of Mississippi, 80
    KKK, 74–75
    law enforcement, 15–16, 17,
      29, 77
    shooting of Meredith, 64
    against sit-in participants, 29
    during voter registration drives,
      51, 53, 54–55
    at wade-in, 31
  see also bombings; murders
Vivian, C.T. (Cordy Tindell)
  Freedom Rides and, 42, 44, 45
  voter registration drive and,
    16–17
voter registration
  barriers to, 50, 51
  drives
    Freedom Summer, 52, 54–56
    intimidation during, 49, 50
    in Selma, 16–17
    strategy of, 48–52
    success of, 52, 56, 57, 94
    violence during, 51, 53, 54–55
  importance of, 46–47
Voting Rights Act (1965), 57, 94

wade-ins, 31
Walker, Ann, 19
Walker, Wyatt Tee, 17–18, 19
Wallace, George, 17, 78–80, 83
"We'll Never Turn Back" (Gober),
   57
"We Shall Overcome," 61
Wesley, Cynthia, 76
West, Ben, 31–33
whites
  excluded from SNCC, 66
  Freedom Riders, 35–36, 37, 40,
    41
  moral responsibility of, 32
  opposed to use of violence, 31
  religious leaders supporting,
    19–20, 44
  sit-in participants, 26, 28, 29
  Southerners
    hostile toward white allies of
      blacks, 50
    sympathizers, 30, 75, 78
  voter registration drive workers,
    49, 54–55
  see also lawmen; violence, by
    whites
Whitten, Jamie, 57
Williams, Adam Daniel, 12
Williams, Hosea, 83
Williams, Robert F., 61–62, 63
Wilson, Albert, 69–70

Young, Andrew, 18, 20
Young, Jack, 44

Zellner, Robert, 55
Zwerg, James, 41

Picture Credits

Cover, AP/ World Wide Photo
AP/World Wide Photo, 15, 64
© Bettmann/CORBIS, 7, 8, 20, 23, 27, 35, 36, 38, 43, 47, 53, 55, 59, 67, 70, 76, 77, 82, 93

© Flip Schulke/CORBIS, 16, 65
© John Springer Collection/CORBIS, 86
Hulton Archive by Getty Images, 30, 73, 88
Library of Congress, 12, 41, 60 ,79

About the Author

Michael V. Uschan has written over thirty books, including *The Korean War*, for which he won the 2002 Council of Wisconsin Writers Juvenile Nonfiction Award. Mr. Uschan began his career as a writer and editor with United Press International, a wire service that provides stories to newspapers, radio, and television. Journalism is sometimes called "history in a hurry." Mr. Uschan considers writing history books a natural extension of skills he developed in his many years as a working journalist. He and his wife, Barbara, reside in the Milwaukee suburb of Franklin, Wisconsin.